# Imperfectly **perfect**

# Imperfectly *perfect*
UNCOVERING THE HIDDEN HAND OF GOD

By: Ryan J. Bradley

Copyright © 2019 by Ryan J. Bradley
All rights reserved. This book or any portion thereof
may not be reproduced or used in any manner whatsoever
without the express written permission of the publisher
except for the use of brief quotations in a book review.

Printed in the United States of America

First Printing, 2019

ISBN 978-1-7336357-0-7

Cover photo taken by Tiffany Marcy

Dedication photo taken by Susan Shea Photography

Book typeset in Minion Pro

Encountering Publications
P.O Box 157
South Hadley, MA 01075

To my son Luke, who has taught me more about myself
and my relationship with God than he
could possibly understand.

# Table of Contents

|    | Preface | ix |
|----|---------|-----|
|    | Introduction | xiii |
| 1  | The Hands On the Clock Just Froze | 17 |
| 2  | Look Out! | 23 |
| 3  | You Can't Bluff a Really Bad Hand | 34 |
| 4  | Which Hand Is Which? | 41 |
| 5  | Sweet Surrender | 52 |
| 6  | Sweet Surrender, pt.2 | 65 |
| 7  | Deaf Ears For an Old Voice | 77 |
| 8  | Hands Waving In the Water | 86 |
| 9  | Anywhere But Normal | 98 |
| 10 | The Wasteland Isn't Wasted Land | 106 |
| 11 | Raise Your Hands! | 114 |
|    | Works Cited | 122 |
|    | About the Author | 124 |

# Preface

When I wrote the manuscript for *Imperfectly Perfect*, Luke was a pretty standard leukemia patient (if such a standard ever really exists). He was an early responder to treatment and was given a high likelihood of cure. But after three years of chemotherapy and one year with his treatments complete, our world collapsed again. Within months after finishing this book, Luke relapsed. Our family was devastated. How could this be? We had come so far, learned so much together, and I was going to use this experience to try and help others connect with God in their hardest moments. How could I have misread the outcome so badly? Our past trial was supposed to stay there, in the past. Lessons were learned, strength was gained, hope had found its champion – so what on earth just happened? Our champion seemed to lay bleeding on the battlefield floor without words or wisdom to revive our broken hearts.

I still remember picking Luke up from school and

having to tell him the results of his blood work. The look on his face could have broken a statue's heart and caused a tear to fall from his mask of mortar. And in an instant we were off to Boston, to Dana-Farber and the Jimmy Fund, to try an experimental treatment that showed hope for cure again. It was in this trial that our world didn't just collapse…it was laid to waste in ruins. If that sounds excessively dramatic, I assure you it's not. It's a story that made doctors cry and rejoice. A story of misery and miracles. A story of pure tragedy that could not squash the last embers of hope from finally igniting again. But that story must wait for a time when I have the courage to write it…when I have the courage to relive it. Until then it remains a paradox, existing both in every waking moment and in the deepest tucked away places of my mind. It's awfully hard to process the trauma of a battle while still in the battlefield, even if your hope for victory seems to have breached the horizon.

Obviously, the release of this book was seriously delayed. For starters, my time became overtaken with hospitals and life-altering decisions. But even more relevant for the present moment, now that the gift of time has arrived, is the question of whether the conclusions I came to in this book even make sense anymore? Are the premises I so diligently tried to capture even real, much less relevant?

What needs to be said in preparation for *this* read is that the meningitis my son contracted during this experimental treatment in Boston, the months in the ICU filled with screaming and horror, the repeated moments watching my son code and be resuscitated, the seizure that lasted for two hours, the pancreatitis, the stroke, the year of brain swelling, the shunt, the 13 neurosurgeries while wondering what would become of the leukemia relapse – they forced me to live out the conclusions and premise of this book in ways I could never have imagined. Not in all my life would I have expected to have to hold these words with a grip so tight it paralyzed my hands. Do the conclusions I came to years before, the ones that became the premise of this book, still make sense? That is one cliff-hanger I can spoil with an answer. They not only make sense, they have become my lifeline. Words of hope that kept me from becoming completely unhinged. I wonder looking back, was writing this manuscript my time of processing the past or my time of preparation for what was to come? I guess, somewhere in the sovereignty of God, it was both.

My prayer as you read this book is that you too will have a chance to process the past…and while I wish no one the pain we have endured, I do pray that perhaps you might even gain a perspective that will prepare you for the future…for life and all the adventures it brings.

# Introduction

I have been asking myself, why did I write this book? What is the real intention here? To wrestle out my own demons in public view? To help others in emotional turmoil? To make sense of my son's battle with cancer and somehow find some deeper meaning in it? I suppose at the core of my desire is the hope that this book might help someone unveil the reality that our situations and circumstances are not always what they appear to be at surface level…even my child's cancer. And that there are many years of survival conditioning that can either lead us to the circumstances we are running from, or at the very least define the way we react to them. I certainly didn't choose my son's illness, but I know for certain the ways I have learned over time to respond to it. In every moment lies this paradox of triumph and tragedy, a competing war of thoughts between "I don't belong here" and "this is a defining moment in my life."

I once knew someone who struggled severely with loneliness - the kind of loneliness that makes the insides feel cold. Unfortunately, she also struggled with profound social anxiety. While psychologically speaking there were many justifiable reasons for her anxiety with people, the end reality is that despite the valid justifications it still left her paralyzed and alone. I asked her one day, "Which is the stronger emotion, the fear of these social situations or the sadness of being alone?" Her response was, "In the moment, nothing is stronger than the fear. But over time, as the moment subsides, nothing is stronger than the sadness." And there lies our dilemma – a slow death or a possible quick one? A certain bout with the cancers of life or a potential stab in the back? This dilemma finds its way into so many facets of life: substances we abuse, relationships we abandon, and opportunities we hide from. Too often we run to the slow death because we think it offers more control, but that is most certainly an illusion. It's the emotional equivalent of being in a rainstorm and refusing to take off our flannel coat to put on a rain jacket for fear of getting wet. I suppose that in the moment of the storm, when one is cold and afraid, it feels more like being in a blizzard and refusing to take off our flannel coat to put on a snow suit for fear of freezing to death in the process. I can understand that instinct and am myself only beginning to learn that there may be another alternative.

And herein lies the point of this book – to aid us in the courageous act of uncovering what was previously hidden from view – that in spite of the storms, many of the moments we fear dying in the cold might actually be opportunities to dance in the rain.

# Chapter 1

## The Hands On the Clock Just Froze

I remember sitting in the waiting area of the emergency room. A feeling like a cloud, gray and hazy, had descended in the room. I couldn't sit still, pacing back and forth, then sitting down, fidgeting in my chair, then pacing back and forth again. I knew. In my heart I knew what it was. I can still see the bruises on his legs, on his back. The faint look in his eyes. The energy it took just to get up. God, why didn't I take him in earlier? How could I not have known that a child shouldn't struggle this hard to do simple every day tasks? The power of the mind to paint its own reality on the canvas of denial...I saw it often as a pastor but now am forced to see it within myself. How did we miss it for weeks at a time? Would that cost him a favorable prognosis? God I can't think this way anymore!

That was pretty much the intensity of the first 48

hours.

What do you do when you have defined your adult life by teaching and preaching faith, and then it walks up and stares you in the face...inches from your brow? All I can tell you is that my life, as well as my family, has been forever changed by the permanent imprint of God's hand in the heartache that is childhood cancer. And I believe I am a better man - a better father, better husband, and better pastor - for it. But my God it hurt. I guess all things worth learning hurt along the way. There is a saying I use in ministry a lot now, whether preaching or counseling. It always goes something like this: "In between the parting of the Red Sea and the arrival at the promised land is a long trip through the desert." If you are unfamiliar with the Biblical story I am referring to, Moses and the Israelites must travel through the wilderness for 40 years after being liberated from slavery in Egypt and after passing through the Red Sea. In that journey, their faith in the God that miraculously saved them from slavery becomes tested as they endure hunger, thirst, and scorching heat on their way to the promised land flowing with milk and honey. In fact, it becomes so discouraging that they grumble how they were better off in slavery where at least they had food. But it is also from this point of despair that God miraculously sustains them with food and water in the desert wilderness. So too for us, we can find ourselves liberated by our faith in God, expecting a life of milk and honey, only to have our faith rocked when we are faced with a long hard road through the desert sands of suffering. But it is here, in those dry parched moments of life, that faith finds its true form and realizes its ability to shape life. It is in these moments that faith changes from something you think about to something you live, something that carries you. It becomes a living faith. A lifeline in moments of peril. Faith grabs your hand, plucks it from the darkness of uncertainty, and unites it to the hand of God.

Look at your hand. Each line in your skin connects with another to make a unique pattern. We learn from grade school that no two fingerprints are identical. A seemingly infinite number of patterns shape our identity and distinguish us from each other, even though at surface glance we all look so similar. While these lines never change, we do. Our identity is shaped in the fires and springs of life. Each of us is a unique series of patterns created from the circumstances of our lives. But those patterns are forever growing; their final picture still unclear.

Now look again. We have callouses from the hard times of life. Thickened skin set there to protect us from the pain we once felt when our flesh was slightly more tender and naive. They seemingly offer a promise that no matter how hard the ball is thrown at us, it will never sting like it did the first time. But it's a myth really. A story we tell ourselves to gain the courage to face our new found fear. Surface pain can be numbed, but the impact is just the same. Behind these callouses are fragile bones that often deny their frailty. So too, the most fragile of us can often appear the roughest at surface level. Hardened by life's pains, they guard their insecurities with a wall of deadened flesh, hoping it will also offer the promise of relief from the curveballs of life.

Look one more time at your hands. They have abilities, some that we may not yet realize. The freedom to grab on or let go, to hold fast or push away. What we push and pull says much about what, or whom, we trust in. It discloses what we ultimately value. Some see only weakness in holding on to someone or something in times of trouble and prefer a "go it alone" strategy. Rugged individualism can be either freedom or slavery to self. Independence is a stone's throw from the idolatry of personhood that fails to see the interconnectedness our hands were made for, in times of both triumph and tragedy. In reality we will all reach out for something to help us manage the peculiarities of life. We will inevitably grab for the security of our own choosing as we face the moments of life's uncertainties. It might come in various forms, shapes, and sizes, but is nonetheless a comfort to deaden the portion of flesh that our callouses can't seem to numb. Yes, we will all reach for something, and it will usually be the first thing grabbed whether in celebration or in grief. But the point of this story is - can your security, whatever form that may be, reach out for you? As sure as we have palms that grab and hold, so too our strength becomes weary and our grip begins to slip through the strains and pains of suffering. And as sure as we have fingers, so it might be that there are things we must let go of before we can grasp the hand that has reached through eternity to grab ours. This story is about the hand of God, and how it comes to us in suffering. How it came to me and my family when my son Luke, just six years old at the time, was diagnosed with leukemia. The story of a hand that grabbed a family struggling before each other's very eyes: myself and my wife Nikki, our two younger sons, Caleb and Eli, who had to watch their older brother suffer, and then, obviously, Luke. Not all parents have to watch their child battle cancer. Most won't ever see that nightmare. But all of us will find moments in our life when we desperately need that hand to come to us. These are the moments when no ordinary hand will do, no casual hand will suffice. These are the moments we need the hand whose stroke paints the silhouette of time.

As may be already evident, this story is not only about childhood cancer. Much of this story is about Luke, but at the risk of being selfish, it's also about me. It's about me as a pastor and as a father, and where those two worlds collided that evening on February 4, 2011 as we sat in the small cell of a hospital room. Above all, this story is about God, and where he is when you're wandering in that long scorching wilderness praying for relief from the noonday sun. So why don't we say this is *our* story - a story of desert sands and water that seems as though it comes from stones on a long and weary road to a new place. It's a destination I didn't even know I needed, and one whose arrival is still a ways off. But I can see the lights of its city in the distance and it keeps me pressing on. I could tell you that this destination is just the end of Luke's battle with cancer, but that's not true. That's a trap really. A trap that takes me right back to the land of slavery, where I am in control and life has a chance to be perfect. No, the place of hope in this story is so much more than that. It is truly a place of freedom. For what I thought our family was being enslaved by, cancer, was in fact teaching us where we were being enslaved by life. God used my son's cancer, in a weird way, to teach us to be free.

It is my hope in writing this book that you, too, might see your own story of control and struggle weaved into the surrounding landscape of this story. Somewhere our hands might even overlap in our common quest to overcome adversity and grasp the most of this wild experience we call life. But above all, my hope is that the hand of God won't seem so far removed in the backdrop of your own cancer - whatever form it takes - because we all have it. There are many metaphors used to describe it, from the scorching desert to the raging seas, but cancer itself is a metaphor. These abnormal little cells of hurt and sorrow, pain and dysfunction, trying to overtake our lives as they seek to divide and conquer. We expend so much energy warring against them, hoping to experience the view from victory, wondering if the battle will ever end. And yet it may be that in the midst of this battlefield, if we pause long enough to stare for just a moment or two, you and I together might catch a glimpse of the lines and callouses on the hand of God.

# Chapter 2

Look Out!
I Can't Hold This Anymore!

God must have a sense of humor. As a pastor I try and show people God loves them even when life throws them those inevitable curveballs. "God doesn't promise us that every pitch in the game of life will be right down the pipe. What he does promise is that he'll teach us how to hit curveballs." I've said that many times, but recently I've had to really hear it for myself. It's as if what I preach and what I live have come sliding into each other. What does it look like? Will I fall apart? Will I grow? Is it chaos? Is it beauty? If I were to sum up a very important lesson I am learning through this process, it's that both chaos and beauty can share the same space sometimes. Maybe they always do.

I have always been an obsessive-compulsive personality. Even as a young child, I would line my presents un-opened on the stairs, or upon opening them spend endless stints of time making sure they were evenly spaced out on the staircase with just the same amount of gap between each toy. I almost drove my parents crazy with it. Actually, I did drive them crazy. They couldn't understand it. I'm not sure I understand it! But I've come to realize that all of our dysfunctions and quirks are there because they are providing something for us. A need is being met. Behind obsessive compulsions is really a quest for control. To hold the foundations of order tightly in your grip. Nothing will blindside you. Life will be seen from every angle...and it will be safe. I suppose it's fair then to say that FEAR is ultimately what drives much of our behaviors. Our lives are, in many respects, dominated by it.

So much of what we say and do, our interactions with people and the masks we wear both in public view and alone in the mirror, are shaped by the fight or flight instincts of fear. There are two foundational concepts I use to set the groundwork when giving pastoral care to someone: 1) behind control is fear, and 2) behind anger is hurt. The counters to these two antagonists are the spiritual groundings of trust and forgiveness. And I do believe they are spiritual concepts at heart. They don't come natural for us, and seem to defy the fight or flight instinct we have embedded in us. For example, if I am the captain of a boat and the first mate is at the wheel when a big storm comes on us, what do I do? I grab the wheel! This is a pretty accurate metaphor for how we handle the storms of our life. Our first instinct is to grab for control. But as we realize the storms of life are beyond our control, feelings like anxiety and depression find root in a common ancestor named stress. It's also where much of my obsessive-compulsive behaviors come from. Trying to organize the pieces of life into its proper boxes, and arranging them in a way that gives me the false security that I am on top of it all. Of course, thinking you're in control of bringing some semblance of order to life is a complete myth. Actually, doing so caused me to ruin beauty in my life far more than it allowed me to see it. Every relationship I had surfaced a tragic flaw, a revealed disorder, a "glitch in the matrix." Other people have a funny way of disrupting our attempts to control life and keep it nestled tightly to our hip.

I finally got to the place in my life where I couldn't take it anymore. I was driving down the road when a pebble popped up from the road and hit my car. The anxiety crept in, "Is there a mark? I must *know*." Obsessive-compulsive disorder can make people appear materialistic about their possessions, but I actually think it's much more about *knowing*. About having a handle on anything that could, or might, or did just happen. So I got out of my car and checked. No mark. Got back into my car. Got back out to check again. Got back in, got back out. And then it hit me like a frying pan to the forehead - I am squeezing the life out of life. Perfection doesn't exist - just enjoy it. And at that moment I did something I still can't believe today. I picked up a stone, swiped it on my car, hopped back in and drove away. Now I *knew*.

What I was really doing in that moment on the side of the road was acting out a lesson I had learned many years earlier, when I was a young boy, though I certainly didn't realize it at the time. I was probably four years old at the time when my father gave me my first radio. Music has always spoken to my soul, so for me, at four years old, it was as if he gave me my first car at sixteen. I took it everywhere with me. But I also obsessed over it, spending each day making sure no one had touched it, and that it was still in the exact position it was when I left it. I stared at it when I came back in the room. The only way I could describe these tendencies is that it was as if I didn't want anything, including the object or the moment, to change. Did everything remain as it was when I last *knew* it? Or had I missed something?

Well, this officially drove my father nuts. He had given me this present hoping I would have fun with it, and instead it was owning me. Enslaving me. He would try to break me out of it by moving the radio an inch out of place with his finger, or at times pretending he was, to which I would respond by asking feverishly, "Did you really move it Dad?" Then I would begin the cycle of spending far too much time trying to find the exact previous location again. Finally, in a moment of desperation, my father picked up the radio and smashed it into pieces on the floor. Gone. Nothing left but a pile of disorder.

Years later, when I was in my early thirties, Dad came up to me and said, "Ryan, there is something I've always felt bad about, and I really need to tell you. Do you remember when I smashed that radio I gave you? I feel horrible every time I think of that." I think my response shocked him, but also gave him some insight into what this disorder was like for me. I replied, "Dad, you don't understand. When you smashed that radio, you liberated me. As soon as it hit the floor, I was free!" I guess that's what I learned to do for myself with the stone that day on the side of the road in my truck.

As funny as these stories sound, they led me down a long and radical rediscovery of self. I had a new motto: "Life was just perfect when it just wasn't perfect." There was a new found freedom in embracing the perfection of imperfection. I literally became perfectionistic about not being perfectionistic. I sought to live life in the comforts of disorder. Clothes...how long will I spend sorting them by color, then by style, then by style and color? But wait are the short sleeve button downs going with the polos or the long sleeve button downs? Ughh! Who cares, they look better to me now in a mess on my floor! Oh the beauty of imperfection! It seemed as though I could touch the outskirts of an intangible contentment. But...it was all still under my control. When compulsions and obsessions crept in, I flew to the radical alternative. That became my mode of operation. If life's "perfection" becomes a mess, blow it up and run. Swipe the stone on the vehicle of life, then get in and drive away. But like I said, God must have a sense of humor. Cancer is awfully hard to smash into pieces on the ground. And it's hard to drive away when it follows you.

Now, as God would have it, I would be forced to swim in the imperfection of life. The reality of life's brokenness would come closer than it ever had to date, and there was nowhere to run. What would I find learning to be present in this mess? Dealing with my son's health is a far cry from sorting Christmas presents and shirts. Would I still see a glimpse of hope while drowning in a wave of fear? I expected I would learn something about my son while watching him fight this battle. I even expected to learn something about God. What I didn't expect is how much I would learn about myself. About the way I defaulted to certain situations and how important control was. I didn't expect to learn how much I had crammed God, the one I proclaimed to be in control, into a little box I had built for him. A box that I could take out whenever I needed. At times I even stood in awe of him, all from the window frame I thought he lived in: my window frame. How this window shows its fragility when it shatters in the hurricane of heartbreak! Then we are left - naked, vulnerable and afraid before our God - with no sill to stoop and gaze from. Only the impulse to cry out, "Save us!"

Salvation can mean many things to us in different points of our life. Sure, we may talk about it in terms of heaven, or a tangible "coming to Jesus" moment after a life of spiritual drought, but there are also times when salvation means the lame man stands and the blind man sees. Times where heaven reaches down and touches the tips of our fingers. For my son, in this journey, salvation means being alive today. For me, salvation is learning not only to find perfection in the mess of imperfection, but to see there's still beauty there if you stick around. If you stay in the messy moments long enough, and hold onto God with all you've got, you can catch a glimpse of it. It shines even brighter when the world looks gray. But you've got to be present. You can't get in the car and drive away. Sometimes you just have to sit with it.

It's not just obsessive-compulsive disorder that reveals where we run and hide. It comes in all forms, and there's bound to be one each of us will recognize. They often stem from the same trigger, but splinter out into different forms that meet our needs in the moment. At least at the surface. For some, this trigger might lead them to a depressed state of aimless drifting. For others, this same trigger might cause the gears in their head to go into overdrive, spinning and mapping a way out into calmer water. I've always defaulted to the anxious mode. Let's rev up the throttle and figure a way out of this storm. This time was different. When there's nowhere to sail to, no throttle within your reach, you feel like all your survival instincts become at that moment useless. There is something in a father that wants to fix problems. I was powerless. I felt so out of place, so confused...the aimless drifter on the open sea. I felt an emotion that seemed foreign to me. An uncomfortable state I couldn't escape from...I felt blue.

Over these last 3 years of Luke's treatment one thing for sure has become quite clear - my wife is the stronger spouse. I was a wreck. I couldn't sit in the hospital for more than 10 minutes with my son before finding my way to the bathroom, to the hallway, to a little nook behind the two doors. Anywhere I could let it all come out. I would just sob...like a young child afraid of what the night might bring. My favorite spot was this little bench seat at the end of the hall outside his hospital room. It looked out over the parking lot where I would watch as people came in and out. Those leaving seemed to have reached a milestone I could only hope for. When would we leave? Would we leave...all of us? I watched as they got into their cars and headed for the free open space of a world whose dark ominous cloud had drifted away in the breeze. The sun seemed to shine for them out there in that parking lot, so I thought. I looked at those who entered into the hospital. "No! Stop! Don't come in, your life may not be the same! Guard yourself with ignorance!" But then reason returned and I remembered that for most of the people coming in, the world was still a safe place.

So many memories surface. The strangest ones seem to linger on. I stumbled across a picture of Luke the other day in his gurney with a mask over his face, trying to have fun on the play deck of the hospital. He was tied to machines and tubes, but I could tell there was a smile lingering under that mask. Other families with sick children were there too. I remember how the conversations usually went. It would start with, "Oh, so what's wrong with your son Luke? Are you expecting to be here long?" The conversation usually ended with a fazed out look, hinting to us that they didn't know what to say when I replied, "He has leukemia." Now maybe there is no truth in what I am about to say, maybe it was just in my head, but to us it felt like in a world of sick children we were "that" family. It feels really self-absorbed to say that. In reality I know there were a lot of really sick kids, perhaps some at that moment with a diagnosis worse than Luke's. We were, and are, fortunate after all. Luke was an early responder to chemotherapy, and no signs of residual cancer were found in his body after the first month. I try and remember to thank God daily (I won't say I never forget). But in that first week at the hospital, this is how it *felt* when our world was flipped upside down. My job as father, my role as the man who once fixed things, was reduced to holding my son down so they could put two very large and very painful needles deep into the tissue of both legs because it is the best known treatment during the start of chemotherapy. What a role I had! Not the role I dreamed about as a father, holding my son in my lap while he screamed in tears, "Why are you doing this to me?"

God, I spent a lot of time on that hallway bench that night. Truthfully, I can't write this now without pausing to search my mind for that parking lot view that took me away...outside myself. It was hands down the lowest point in my life. I remember crying out on that little 4-foot bench seat, "God, I need you now! Please don't leave me! I can't do this without you. Luke needs you so bad right now. We all do! Teach us how to live with this!" As I sit here today writing, I can say with certainty that God never left me. He carried me when I couldn't lift my head to see the road in front of me. He is faithful, even in the darkness. I know this not just because I read it in the Bible or learned it in theology class during seminary. I know because I've lived it. Because I flailed in darkness and he grabbed my hand. God's hand was never more visible than it was in this pain. And that's the point of this book. That's the story I want to share.

Where is God when it hurts? He is closer than the shirt on your back. But that can be hard to see sometimes because there are inner reasons we keep God at bay. There is a survival instinct that, with a hard push away, tries to keep God removed from the reigns of our life. For as much as we may ask God to be there for us, our actions betray us. They hint at a truth we probably would never admit - that we prefer God to stay at a distance that seems more familiar. In times of fear and pain, don't we always search for comfort and the familiarity of "normalcy"? Well, what if that normalcy is not the life God had intended for us? What if God would use even the moments of suffering to draw us closer to him? What if we, in a search for control and normalcy, with a conditioned survival mode we didn't even know was there, pushed away the very hand we asked to carry us? It just might be that it takes something like childhood cancer for us, for me, to realize that our hands can't contain all the heaviness of life. As quickly as our hands look to grab the wheel of control, hoping to put back the pieces of normalcy, we are confronted with the reality of a world that is beyond what our hands can hold. And there is God. Surely he has been there for a while, and yet only now can I see the lines of his palm. He has never been this close. At least not that I could see. Maybe that is the difference.

Remember the old children's song, "Jesus loves me this I know, for the Bible tells me so." There is a story about that song and a well-known theologian named Karl Barth. As the story goes, a student at the University of Chicago asked Barth if he could summarize all his life's theological findings into one sentence. Barth responded by quoting this famous opening line from the song. "Jesus loves me this I know, for the Bible tells me so." As touching as this story is, I would like to add a new line of my own if I may be so bold. Jesus loves me this I know, for when I cried out he never let go. These are the experiences of life where those stories in the scriptures are weaved into our own story. Where God is not only the God of the pages, but the God of life, who lives and acts just as he did in times of old. The God who is the same yesterday, today, and tomorrow. One whose hand is right there in the darkness, breaking through the clouds of eternity to grab hold of us and pull us near. A God whose hand does not let go!

Do you know God from this place of desperation? Have you ever cried out to God, for fear or anger, but mostly because you were desperate to feel his grip fasten around your palms? Some say we shouldn't go to that place. That it lacks a sophistication and refinery they confuse with reverence. Instead they insist our relationship with God has to be some sterile formality, like a student in the principal's office, hoping to say the right thing to avoid consequence. But what if that advice wasn't right at all? What if it was okay to come before God afraid and an absolute wreck? Could you do it? Could you come unglued and trust that the pieces would be put back together again? Maybe you would find that not only will God embrace you just as you are, but for that moment in time…you might even be just perfect.

# Chapter 3

## You Can't Bluff a Really Bad Hand

I had plans. I was taking this family somewhere. The vision was etched in the landscape of my imagination. My job was going well, the church was growing. My wife, Nikki, had employers who were looking to bring her up into management. We were living in a nice antique home with a rent to buy option. Things seemed to be heading on the right path. The pursuit of the American Dream while pursuing God's calling - all rolled up into one pretty package! One that I could set on the stairs and adjust its position when needed, just like I did as a child on Christmas morning. "You're being too worldly Ryan, a little to the right. OOPS, now you're too focused on church, just a little to the left. Not too much! You don't want to lose yourself!" The back and forth between the spiritual and worldly life is not only dizzying, it's not what God calls us to. He calls us to an authentic life with faith intertwined in the fabric of our being, unable to come apart as faith supports life and life breeds faith.

I am not saying I was phony, in fact, I think the growth of our church has always had its roots in being genuine. I certainly wasn't living two different lives... but in some ways I guess I was. My sermons and messages were the result of intentionally seeking God's voice. I submerged myself in God for the "church stuff." I relied on him and was certain that if he did not sustain and equip me, I would flounder. But I wonder if I approached the rest of my life that way? My family? Friends and other relationships? This life is filled with many callings, a pastor being one of them for me. But had I given my role as husband and father wholeheartedly to God, and relied on him to sustain and equip me in the personal aspects of my life? Or was I still trying to sustain myself, seeking control so that my vision could become my reality? If I am honest, I would say the latter. Many people would say God plays a more dominant role in their private lives than their job. For me it was the opposite. I was so engrossed in it as a pastor, I think it faded as a husband and father. I could sit and pray with people in my office about their hurts, fears, and hopes, but at home prayer became part of my "good parent's 'to-do' list."

Then cancer showed up. I still remember the doctor's words, "Mr. & Mrs. Bradley, we have confirmed - it is leukemia." It was as if the disease sprung to life, with a face pale and gray like the kind you see in older horror movies. He had knocked on the door of our lives and forced his way into our home, and though not welcome, he just wouldn't leave. He followed us around constantly for the first few months, peering at us from the corners of our home, jobs, and social activities, reminding us that he was still there, as were all the possibilities he represented.

Back around the same time as I was having grand visions of the American Dream, Luke was showing his first interest in sports. I think of all the activities you can do in sports, my absolute favorite is playing catch. Just two people - a father and son, two close friends, family members reuniting at a gathering - talking about life while throwing a ball. There is something pure about it. It's a time where hopes are shared, secrets slip out, frustrations find sympathy and hurt finds empathy. A time when the complexities of life are boiled down to their simplicities. If you've ever seen *Field Of Dreams*, you'll remember the pinnacle of the movie when [spoiler alert] after years of guilt and hurt over their relationship, the main character asks his father, "Hey dad, you wanna have a catch?" It was as if all the pains of the past were healed in that one act.

The first summer after Luke's diagnosis was the hardest. It was the most intense time of chemotherapy. They call it "delayed intensification". This is the period when his hair fell out, his face was swollen, and he looked every bit the cancer patient. This was the time when my "Hey dad, you wanna have a catch?" moment was taken from me. What right do I have to lament the loss of a game of catch when my son was losing so much more? I know it seems selfish, but I would rather be honest with how I felt because in the end feelings aren't always about right or wrong. They are the way we process change, handle grief, and fight through fears. I had longed for those times of playing catch with my son as he grew. I waited for those moments. They were supposed to be here now. But the medication affected his stance, the way he ran, his ability to catch and throw, never mind the complete lack of energy and struggle to focus while in the "chemo fog". He went from fast and tall to slow and the shortest in his class. Catching the ball became for me a painful reminder that others were growing differently than he was.

It was never about some fairy tale dream of him becoming a professional athlete. I just wanted to have a catch. To watch him grow. I didn't want to watch him in bed throwing up blood. I wanted to fix up scrapes on his knees, not sores in his mouth. I wanted to yell from the back yard, "Head for the end zone Lukey, the crowd is on their feet for the final play of the game...TOUCHDOWN!" I would eventually get that moment, but in a very different way, for a very different reason. Victory would not be in the drama of an imaginary game but in the nail biting thriller of real life. And the "touchdown" would be a much sweeter prize!

But that day was three years off in the distance. It seemed at the time like an island we were rowing to, but could not yet see because it was just too far off. So I guess we'll say for now that our sport became rowing. And row we did! Altogether as a family. Mostly Luke had the oars, but when he was too tired to keep pushing for that island, we grabbed the oars and pulled with him.

I remember one afternoon we were outside in our yard, and he sat down on the ground and finally said *it*.

"Dad, why did I have to get cancer?" This was the only time I had ever heard him say it, and the only time I ever would. He never brought it up again...never complained...never got mad at God. Just this one time of exasperation at what was happening to him and that was all. I didn't have a long in depth theological answer. Something about the word "Dad" introduced the question differently than I had heard it the many times before in my office.

I've never been a big fan of "heady" theological answers to people's pain anyway. They just aren't helpful in the moment no matter how much truth they might hold. Still, when these kinds of questions begin with "Pastor Ryan," you somehow feel your role is to help people sustain their faith in hard times, rather than just sit with them in the pain of it all. You leave those bedside visits hoping they found encouragement, which is certainly not a bad thing on its own, but it also fills a need in you as a pastor. A need to be needed. Again, there is nothing wrong with the desire to help, still, I wonder if the desire to have them be encouraged didn't cause me to miss their desire to just simply be heard and told they're loved. And then Luke asked me the question. That question. When that question has "Dad" in front of it, it sounds so different. That one word can change the tone, the way it's heard, its impact, and my desired response. All I wanted to do was hold him. To keep his head close enough to my chest that he wouldn't see my tears. I didn't have a thought of being profound. I didn't want to be the one with an answer, because for the first time I didn't want to be the one who was asked the question. Not with the word "Dad" in it. "Pastor," fine. But this question can't start with the word "Dad." Not my son.

I know that in this whole journey with Luke, the driving force behind anything my wife and I said or did was love. But, oh, is it a love that hurts sometimes! A love that takes all your rehearsed answers and sweeps them up as worthless rags. All I could bring myself to say was, "I don't know buddy. I don't know why this happened. But you keep fighting it and you'll be back up and running again. And someday God is going to use you. Look at me son. Listen to me. With all you'll have learned from this whole thing, you're going to be strong in ways others have never experienced. God is going to use this." This answer was not given behind a closed office door. It didn't have to journey across an oak desk to be heard. It was said in the field of dreams - just a father and son sitting in the grass with his head leaned up against mine. I guess it was his way of saying, "Hey dad, you wanna have a catch?"

A moment of total honesty. I was hesitant to put God in my response to Luke's question. Not because I didn't trust God. I was trusting him like I never had before. I was searching for the hand of God in the forefront of the hand we had been dealt...the hand Luke had been dealt. And Luke's prognosis was great. But there is always the lingering "what if." If I told him it was all in God's hands, as I have in the past to encourage people's faith in dark moments, and something went horribly wrong...would it shatter his young innocent faith? It's one thing for me to trust God's hand, but how do I communicate it to my son when I don't know the outcome of the hand we are facing? I know

God doesn't promise us that this world will be void of heartache. The rain falls on all of us. If that turn happened, how could he confront death while feeling abandoned by God? How would he reach for a hand he might think had left him? That thought almost buckled me. But at that exact moment, when Luke asked "the question" and I was faced with the reality of God's hand intertwined with the hand of cancer, faith was found in telling my son that God was going to use this in his life. Faith wasn't a fancy doctrine filled with the most logical reasoning for the Christian claims. It was a word at a moment where time seemed to stand still. It didn't demand a response from a textbook. It was a response given when a father and son are holding on to God's hand with all they've got...together.

I had plans you know. I was taking this family somewhere. But it's amazing how things change when a question starts with "Dad."

# Chapter 4

## Which Hand Is Which?

Did I do something wrong, God? Funny, my son is the one suffering and I am the one assuming punishment. Actually it's not funny, it's sad. A sad testimony of how we so often view God. Not in a million years would I counsel people this way as their pastor, and yet it seems to be a gut human reaction when you're actually the one experiencing hurt. God's hand seems like it reaches down from the sky with fire shooting behind it, swinging forcefully in our direction, getting ready to strike us down for our crimes. We cringe and cower like a child getting ready to endure a blow from a parent whose anger has turned to unbridled rage. Is this our God? Stop and think about that for a moment. Close your eyes if you have to, but envision the hand of God. What does it look like? Is it something you reach out for with every bit of strength you can muster, or something you run from as soon as it appears? What projection from your imagination becomes painted on the surrounding landscape? Are people running in fear and trembling, or flocking to be sheltered and embraced? Is it dark with storm clouds swirling, or are they dispersing into a sanctuary of beauty and peace? See the underlying question of this book, "Where is God when it hurts?" begins first with the question, "*Who* is God when it hurts?"

Much of how we answer the question of who God is relates to the associations we have of what God does and how he comes to us in our times of distress. How do we view the hand of God, as one that helps us, or one that hurts us? One that punishes, or one that rescues? How we answer that will inform much of how we see God's hand in suffering. It's a question that reveals a lot of who we think God is and how he responds to our desperation. When we leave the pews and find ourselves in the middle of the desert, who do we really believe God is? The one who sits upon the mountain waiting to inflict cosmic consequence with bolts of lightning, or the one who dwells in the wastelands to restore beauty?

It's not that I don't think God corrects or disciplines us. I do. On more than one occasion I have felt God's hand repositioning my life to fall in alignment with him (which has not always been a pain free experience). But that was far more the result of my resistance to God's hand than it was his blow to my cheek. Like a kid who knows he's done wrong, I would avoid God as I redefined what was "right for me". I didn't want to face one whose standards I was dismissing. Of course, that lasted until my new standards ran me aground and life seemed a big mess. Then I would shy my way back, wondering if God would still be there for me, which of course he always was. The words the late Lane Staley sang in "River of Deceit" say it best - sometimes our "pain is self chosen."

Still we must be careful not to confuse "you reap what you sow" with "the hand of God in suffering," because more often than not God's hand holds for us that which we did not sow nor had any expectation of reaping. Meaning this, that God's hand in my life, stretched out and accessible, has ultimately been a source of healing and redemption not pain and punishment. And it has been most certainly undeserved on my part. That's why we call it grace. But no matter how often God's hand graciously restores and lifts us to higher ground, it seems we still find ourselves waiting for it to strike us down in the end. Maybe because deep inside we feel we deserve it? Maybe it's because of our ultimate fear of death? Even to the mind whose hope is in the hereafter, death seems so final. A judgment of discard for all our flaws and brokenness. Death is often viewed as God's final answer as judge, jury, and executioner. The very word strikes both fear and curiosity, terror and intrigue. What is out there...beyond it? We may dare to ask, "Is death really God's final answer, or is there something more? Is it God's hand of doom, or his hand lifting us to a place beyond all this hurt, brokenness and suffering?" As ironic as it sounds, the finality of death seems so...infinite. The very concept is the closest our minds can get to something eternal. And in this mindset God resumes his position as the god of lightning bolts, and redemption is reserved for a hope that lies only beyond the grave. No wonder that on this side of heaven we see God's hand as one of judgment. We have limited his redemptive touch to the life hereafter, and believe what we reap in this life must surely have been sown. Even if we wouldn't think of saying it this way, the thought surfaces at the most inopportune times.

My mother lost her father when she was 14 years old in a tragic construction accident in Hartford, Connecticut. My grandmother never talked much about the passing of her husband, but every time "The Old Rugged Cross" was played in church she would weep in the pew. I remember that vividly about her. Something of the pain still lingered deep within her soul. Not much was said about it, but it was there. Some places within us can't help but sneak out from time to time. It was after a sermon I preached on suffering that my grandmother, filled with salty eyes approached me and said, "My first thought when it happened was 'were we being punished?'" I knew what she was referring to. She didn't have to explain. She spoke again, "Then I thought, what am I going to do? And by the time I had taken a step forward in the hospital it hit me, I have to accept it and keep this family going."

Why do we think tragedy is our punishment? Is it the "action = consequence" nature of our relationships we have learned since childhood? Maybe we are all waiting in the back of our minds for our lusts and lies, selfishness and shame, greed and gluttony to catch up to us in the end. Maybe down deep we think it should. Perhaps we walk as children, aware of our own misgivings and awaiting our discipline, listening behind the throngs of other noises for the bell to chime and the hand to strike. But aren't we told that God is a god of mercy, whose love knows no bounds? Can you actually envision striking your own child with such a blow that it devastates the rest of their lives, wreaking permanent tragedy for their disobedience? If not, what does that say about the way we think of God? Perhaps we read that he is the God of mercy but view our experiences with him as a god of lightning bolts and volcanoes!

When you are grasping for answers, the guilt that's been banished to the furthest recesses of our mind can explode with magnum force into the forefront - rational or irrational. For as many times as I have held people's hands at their bedside or in the pew of their loved one's funeral, and told them God is not punishing them, that he will get them through this hard time, I guess I am shocked at how easily the same thoughts crept up in me. I shouldn't be surprised though. I've always been waiting for the cluttered colors of my shortcomings to be sorted out. And anytime I've lifted my hand to do it, it's been a painful process that I had to finally blow up and drive away from. Why should God's hand be any different? I've always had expectations of people that were out of reach, none more than those I've laid on myself...and those I realize now I've laid on God. I wonder if I haven't confused the two of us?

Or maybe I've wrapped God up and packaged him into the image of my father? Down deep, it just may be that I'm waiting for the hand of God to smash the objects of my attention into a thousand pieces on the ground. It's shocking at how often people fashion God into the image and likeness of their parents, especially their father. They don't even realize it, but as they tell you of their relationship with God (hopes and struggles), and then tell you about their relationship with their father, it becomes clear that the two have become tangled. That intertwining can be awfully hard to untangle. But it's so important! Otherwise, when the hand of God comes to us, we might pass right by, or push it away, confusing it for someone else's. He may use us as parents, but his fingerprints are still his own. God wants us to know him for who he is - not who we've crafted him to be. My father is a wonderful man, and we are extremely close, but God he is not. Nor would he want to be. As fathers, the most valuable lesson we can teach our children is how to reach for God's hand, even as they let go of ours.

Now with that said, I'd like to offer yet another reason as to why we often associate tragedy and heartache with punishment. One that goes deeper than our guilt. What if it's just another form of control? Sounds like an odd statement, I know. If it is God inflicting punishment, how does that put us in control? For many of us, however, "God" is just another way of projecting our own quest for control. We know our limitations, and so God becomes the vehicle through which we exercise our own authority and significance. If something so momentous as cancer can be the outcome of my action, something I did wrong in the past, then I certainly would have an enormous amount of influence in the world. Better to have it the result of our own action than be victim to the stroke of chance right? And here's where it gets more complicated: maybe...just maybe...if our actions caused it, we can also undo it?

Herein lies my form of insanity over the last 3 years. Don't laugh! If ministry has taught me anything over the years, it's that we all have a touch of insanity rolling around in that head of ours! In fact, I actually had a sign hanging over my office door that read "Embrace Your Insanity." My form of it over the last three years has been, "Things are going really well, prognosis is good - can I blow this?" I'd better be on my best behavior so God doesn't turn this in another direction. Any temptation that crept in my head, whether I want to admit it or not, found its way into this anxiety. It may not have lasted for long bouts all the time, but it was there. I may never have actually thought we were being punished with Luke's diagnosis, but I certainly had internal battles over whether my ongoing shortcomings could lead me outside of God's blessing and change the prognosis. Oh the power in my hands! Oh the control I have!

Of course I didn't really feel powerful. I felt trapped. Helpless. And these thoughts weren't something I shared with others. They weren't rational. They weren't even constant. They floated in and out of my head, seemingly trailing my temptations, as a reminder of my desire to control and failure at being perfect enough to live out my "bargains" with God. If I gave into temptation, I would start my plea with God. "Lord, don't think I am ungrateful for all you've done with Luke. I'm sorry I messed up again."

To anyone who reads this and says, "how self-obsessed!" - I say you're absolutely right! You have unmasked the depth to which something like childhood cancer can shake your insecurities, rattle the loose bolts in your head, and make you re-assess your foundations. It owns you for a bit. Fear owns you. Again, when people came into my office and asked if God was punishing them, the answers I gave them looked nothing like the questions I began asking when cancer found its way to my son. And unfortunately, this attempt at "influencing God through my behavior," even if irrational and for only short spells of helpless insanity, was really just another tour in the quest for perfection. My old method of finding order without error, and keeping all things in their place, had disguised itself and found its way into my most desperate of moments.

But I am not the only one. I think most of life is about control. Maybe not everyone would admit that, but it's there in one form or another. It may not come as obsessive-compulsive behavior or perfectionism, but control will always find a vehicle to run our lives. Stemming from the reality of a world filled with uncertainty and the lingering fear of loss, it guides our interaction with the world. The world is always changing, and change sooner or later deals us a losing hand. Where there is life, there is death. That reality is too much for us to bear. So we dare to think, "If only I could control the outcomes." Or at the very least, "How can I orchestrate things enough so I am not taken by surprise?" It's a maddening quest, this search for control. It almost defines our existence. Look for it and you will find it - in governments and in churches, in schools and in social centers. Sex and money has often been thought of as the ultimate ends of all human striving, but they are merely pawns in the quest for control. Keep looking and you will see it in all walks of life. Even depression and anxiety can be seen through the lens of control. They start as survival instincts, self-defense mechanisms we use to shield us, numb us, or keep us from being caught off guard. But they can end up enslaving us.

I have seen many people in my office who are most certainly unaware that they are using and holding onto depression as much as depression is holding onto them. It has become a seemingly safe default, almost comfortable in its uncomfortability. It wraps us in a familiar persona, gives us a reason to disconnect from the world and people we view as dangerous to our emotional well-being. It may stem from a fear about the insecurity of life and relationships, but it progresses to a form of mental illness that chains us by serving a need in us to feel emotionally safe. Depression can be a way of controlling our emotional engagements that in the end controls us. It comes to us like an old friend, promising a relationship of rest for our weary souls, until it begins to devour and ravage our inner most being.

Anxiety, in this respect, is not much different. As mentioned earlier, one can view anxiety and depression as two outcomes of a common source - stress. In anxiety, the need to unplug from perceived pain takes a back seat to the desire to stay on top of any possible pain that may come our way and prepare for it before it strikes. Replaying all possible scenarios in our head or thinking of ways we can affect the outcome if we are quick enough to act, all of this is a form of control. We may not be aware of it consciously, but it is an attempt to deal with this tricky situation we call life. It is a way we learn to survive. How cautious are our lives! How damaging the emotional stress left in the wake of life's fragility!

Husbands and wives, parents and their adolescent teens, co-workers - there is no safe haven from the inner struggle for control. But keep looking farther. Look deep and you will even find it in a place much closer to home. Peel up the floorboards of the life you have built for yourself and you will see it lying there. If your search is honest and true, you will find the desire for control staring you in the eye with a calloused smile. You will find it within yourself. Affecting you more than you realize. Control is both what we strive for and what we are frustrated by. But to give up the quest would be to blaspheme our ultimate idol - the self. And herein lies the deepest lesson my son's leukemia has taught me - I AM NOT IN CONTROL!

None of us are. Does that frighten you or sound blissfully restful? Perhaps a combination of both feelings that swing back and forth seemingly with no rhyme or reason. I have grown over time to realize the importance of this question, and the more time goes by, the more important this question becomes. Does control, or lack of control, bring the greater peace? I suppose it depends on your point of view, and on whether you think that your lack of control means the world is uncontrollable. Is there a governing hand greater than your own that can intervene when yours can't? Is the world utter chaos left for you to put in order, or is there a hand that makes sense of it all…even when it doesn't make sense to you? If you stop right now as you read, and think about where you spend the most energy trying to control life, there's a good chance that lying there next to you is also your biggest ball and chain.

# Chapter 5

## Sweet Surrender

"Sweet surrender" is a term that comes to life once you've experienced it. When a burden has been released of its crushing weight and your arms begin to feel the burn subside, there is a sweetness in letting go. We usually don't associate surrender with anything pleasurable or profitable. Certainly not sweet. It's an action we've reserved for moments of defeat and the humility of loss. We expect to come away with our heads low on the ground prepared to have something valuable - a freedom perhaps - taken from us.

In part, I suppose this is true. Our freedom is limited, or at the very least revealed to be illusory. The realization that we are not in control shatters our concept of freedom and we feel powerless to resist the onslaught of life's unfolding. On horses and chariots life's antagonists have pursued us, that we might bow before them in defeat. But a strange turn of events occurs when we finally reach the end of ourselves. Instead of surrendering to the slings and arrows of misfortune, we turn and surrender before the only one left standing. We surrender to God. "Take this battle because I'm hurt and broken! Lift me, my legs feel bruised and battered!" It is a humbling moment to be sure, an exasperated moment, but not a moment of defeat. Instead of being left desolate, we come out having gained something. We gain a deeper understanding of our relationship with God. We begin to see who we are, and who he is, in the battles life has strategically placed before us.

Psalm 34:8 says of God, "Oh, taste and see that the Lord is good! Blessed is the man who takes refuge in him!" (English Standard Version). This verse also comes alive once you've experienced it. Once you encounter God in suffering, the words begin to jump from their pages to take their stand. The sweet taste the psalmist refers to is an encounter he has with God that allows him to know God differently than he had before. It encouraged his faith and left him confident in the one who would comfort him. Whatever this experience was, we can be pretty certain it didn't stem from abundance and prosperity. It came from moments he was forced to take refuge. His "tasting" came from the place of sweet surrender, where the events of life led to the need for shelter.

The word refuge means shelter or protection. It is a place where we hide away when the storms of life try to drown us out. In the times of greatest suffering, God's hand extends the closest to us. The lower we sink, the farther God's hand reaches - never out of grasp. Indeed, if the battle has left us crippled beyond the ability to reach for his hand, God scoops us up to carry us. It is from this point that the most spiritual of all acts begins to germinate within us. Once we see the hand of God as carrying us, not punishing us, he becomes the one we run to, not the one we run from. He becomes our refuge...our sweet surrender. But first we have to get to the end of ourselves. We must reach that point that causes us to smash down the idol of our own self-determination. That towering golden cathedral of the self, filled with monuments constructed to the glory of our own will. That is the surrender part. That is the hard part.

My sweet surrender came a good year and a half after Luke's diagnosis. Sure, I cried out to God in the beginning. I spent time pouring my heart out to him and showing our need for his hand. But I never relinquished control in a way that allowed my dependence on God to free me from the weight I was carrying. This weight was the fear of uncertainty. Instead I looked for signs of what would become of my son. It seemed that there were signs at every turn, popping out to keep me alerted to what might be happening. Of course, they weren't *all* real signs. They were my way of keeping some control, making sure the rug wouldn't pull out from under me before I had a chance to brace for the fall. On more positive days, I held on to signs that filled me with hope. On bad days, well...those just weren't good days at all. My head would shuffle aimlessly between good indicators and bad - "Doctor seemed positive today" or "Blood counts were low again, what could it mean?" I suppose this shuffling back and forth between being confident and concerned is normal, but it also gets dizzying. It began to feel a lot like moving toys on a staircase - back and forth to the left and the right, looking for just the right picture to capture what truly "is" before me. I just couldn't let it go. I glued myself to these would-be signs as if they were a forecast, letting us know if we should run for shelter or play in the park.

Above all others, there were three signs in my mind - two frightful and one hopeful - that I replayed over and over again, exploring their complexities and searching for their hidden meanings as if they held clues to the road ahead. The first one actually happened a year before Luke was even diagnosed. I was a chaplain doing my Clinical Pastoral Education at Baystate Hospital in Springfield, MA. In this internship, we as chaplains would make visitation rounds, offer spiritual care for those who requested it, and respond to emergencies that were surely traumatic for the families involved. For whatever reason, my shifts seemed to coincide with a lot of tragedies and deaths involving children. The first two murders of the year in Springfield were both teenagers who were brought into the emergency room while I as on call. Infants and newborns, twins who passed away at birth, fathers who had young children, teens with their whole lives ahead of them - these were the dominant shifts I encountered during this internship. All of them seemed to reinforce this underlying fear we have as parents of being separated from our children. During this time, I would go to sleep at night in the chaplains' quarters praying that the pager would not go off to wake me with the reality of another dead child.

All the chaplains dealt with heartache, and I certainly don't want to minimize what they went through as well, but I seemed to get more than the normal lot. It was beginning to be obvious to the other people in our program, to the point where one chaplain was concerned I was going to get burned out from the ministry before I really even got going. I remember vividly my supervisor coming up to me and asking, "You've really had a lot to process. Have you gone to God and asked why you seem to be getting so many deaths involving children?" My answer is still framed in big black inscription, bold and daunting in my memory: "I hope God is not preparing me for something with my own child someday." I will never forget that response, especially not now. It is etched on a gravestone erected by my own imagination, haunting me for the last three years since Luke was diagnosed. Was it a sign? Were you trying to show me something God? This can't be your hand of fate, can it? Can your hand be reversed, change directions…chart a new course? Please God, where else can I go to but you to change this? What other hand is there but yours?!?

The second sign also occurred before Luke was diagnosed, this time by about three months. It involved a song Luke wrote and asked if I would record for him in my home music studio. Now maybe I am biased, I know most kids make up songs when they are six years old, but this was different. This song seemed to come from somewhere both deep within and far beyond. It went like this:

I am home,

> not the home on the ground
> I am in his house,
> not the house on the ground
> I am home where I belong,
> and I am in the Lord's house
> He is the one who made me,
> and he is the one who gave me life
> He is the one who made me,
> and he is the one who will let me fall
> ...Let me fall

You might read this and think, "Okay, this clearly came from a kid who has been overly entrenched in religion to the point where he can't be normal. Kids don't write songs like that." And you would be only partially right. Kids normally don't write songs like that. Adults don't normally write songs like that. But our family is not the Flanders household from The Simpsons. Our boys know all the latest shows and sing all the latest songs. They are certainly taught our faith, but aren't sheltered from the world they are growing up in either. They get into trouble from time to time, at home and school, much to their parent's chagrin. I don't want to minimize the role that our faith plays in our lives, because it is very dominant, but neither will I minimize the "out of the blue, seemingly other-world-like" appearance of this song from Luke. It was so beautiful and so deep for a 6-year-old boy. But there was one part that disturbed me. So I asked Luke, "What do you mean by 'God will let you fall'?" His response stunned me. It shook me really. He replied as carefree as could be, "God made me and so he will also let me fall to the ground and die. That is when I'll go to heaven." As morbid as it sounds, I swear there was such an innocence and tenderness in his voice...a confidence even... that it left me speechless. In my child, there was more of a complete trust in the hand of God, a total relinquishing to the will of God, than I can ever remember having myself. In one statement, Luke had shown more surrender than I could muster in a lifetime. It was, for him, just a simple fact. God's hand was in everything, so everything was okay. Even death. It was sweet surrender.

Jesus told his followers that they must come to God like a child. Pastors and preachers, theologians and teachers, all have described Jesus' words in different ways. From explanations of childlike innocence, to discourses on the ability of a child to believe without doubt what they are told, this scripture has been used to make a point in countless sermons. But for me, this verse will forever remind me of a child's ability to trust the hand of God. It is a verse synonymous now with sweet surrender. But it frightened me.

Three months. Three months before cancer and these were the lyrics Luke wrote. How many times I went back to that song and asked God those same questions again. Is this a sign of what is to come? Were you trying to tell me something...prepare me...prepare Luke?!? I couldn't even sing the song in my head because it was too "in my face" with a possibility I didn't dare stare down. But it lunged at me in the most inconvenient of times. In the late night hospital beds and tearful mornings it took its aim at me, taunting me with cruel threats and obscene gestures. To this day I have still not had the courage to put that recorded version back into the CD player of my truck. His moment of sweet surrender became my worst nightmare. How odd, this disconnect. How strangely twisted, this saga of life that unfolds. Sometimes you really do feel like the world is a stage. But we are not *only* the actors. No...instead we waver between actor and audience, unable to tell at times which is which. Are we watching the story play out...or living it? So as the song crept in to play its chimes in my head, I forgot its lyrics. It became for me only a melody. One that, when the lyrics were removed, took me back to its original innocence and beauty. And from there I could have faith in one thing above all others - the hand of God was at work in my son. That I was sure of.

Those two signs were the ones that frightened me the most. They crowded me in a corner and taunted me with the fragility of life. There is, however, one sign that I've hung on to more than the others. This third sign has been for me a place of refuge. When fear crept in, this is the place I ran to in my head. It is, I believe, a place of God.

In the year before my son's diagnosis, one of the young married couples in our church lost their baby girl, Eva, due to a rare but deadly neurological disorder. I offered emotional and spiritual support as best I could, but still I knew the pain was unbearable for them. It was a restless place of discontent that only time and the hand of God could heal. But the way God brought a pivotal piece of that healing process was indeed extraordinary. Eva's mother, Sadie, had been praying (unknown to me at the time) that God would use her in some way, to serve him as a way out of the sadness and grief she felt over her loss. Her nightly prayer was, "God give me a way of serving you. A way to help someone who also needs healing. I need to be used by you, to see and be part of your work, so I can be encouraged too. How can I serve you in the midst of such great pain?" It's quite natural to look for meaning and purpose in the wake of tragedy. And while these feelings may be natural, the way God answered her prayer was supernatural.

When Sadie first heard about Luke's diagnosis, she went to God immediately in prayer. "Lord, I don't want to see another child hurting. Heal him God!" At that moment, an intense feeling of God's presence came to her and she heard a voice in her head say distinctively and clearly, "It's already done. Start coming in gratitude now for the healing I am already doing." Now I want to be clear about two things at this point. First, "It's already done" does not mean we stopped chemotherapy or held our son from treatment. For all I know, it may not have meant that the cancer was gone that instant. Perhaps, it meant that things were already set into motion for Luke's recovery? Or maybe that the two medications Luke had already received at that point did their job? Or perhaps it meant simply that God had healed him supernaturally in the moment? I don't claim to know, but I do, however, believe in the power of prayer and in the power of God to heal. That doesn't mean we void our responsibilities as parents. God can use doctors and medicines, or anything he wants for that matter, to apply his healing hand to any situation. But in the end, in whatever capacity God chooses, we were depending on *HIS* healing hand.

Secondly, Sadie is not an "I hear voices" type of person, and at that time was feeling the most uncertain about God's role in healing given the outcome of her daughter's life. For her, this experience was a first. She does not walk around the church saying, "The Lord told me..." Up until this point, I actually knew her as a bit reserved. But she felt this presence and voice from God so strongly that it drove her from her shell to speak what she was feeling. My father, also a pastor at that time, stood before the church the Sunday after Luke was diagnosed to ask for prayer. When it came time to ask for prayer for his grandson he just stood there... unable to speak...choking back his tears with his voice quivering. Many people knew what was going on, and before he knew it there were people coming forward to put their arms around him. At that moment, Sadie locked eyes with my father and said, "It's going to be okay. It's already taken care of. Trust me, I know this. I know it in here (pointing to her heart)." Knowing Sadie the way I do, I can't imagine what power came over her to speak that boldly, especially to one of her pastors in the middle of a worship service. Actually...I do know what power that is. It is the powerful hand of God that reaches down and moves us when we cry out to him. Somewhere between a mother's prayer to be used in the wake of loss, and a family's crying out for their little boy to be healed - the hand of God moved.

   Months later, as tests showed great results and Luke was labeled an "early responder" to the chemotherapy, Sadie would tell me that a strange thing occurred in her during all of this. Luke found healing. But Sadie also found healing. Her prayer to be used in the outgoing tide of her lament had been answered, and a renewed confidence in God came with it. A confidence that reassured her of where her baby Eva is - in that very hand of God she just felt move on her. The hand that came strong and swift, with the assurance of a power beyond the five senses we have come to rely on in this world. The hand that came soft and tender as it picked her up and set her gently down on new ground.

That same Sunday afternoon, after church, I called Sadie from the hospital to thank her for the words she passed on. Her voice, slightly shaky from the experience, answered, "Ryan, I am glad you called. I wanted to tell you something that I know in my heart. I feel it as strong as I ever have felt anything in my life. Eva was meant to be healed in God's arms, up in heaven. But Luke was meant to be healed here." This, above all others, was the sign I clung to. Whenever I was scared. When the morbid pale-faced man peered his head around the corners of my life, stalking me, hoping to see me buckle - the shaky but strong voice that talked to me that day repeated her line in my mind, "Eva was meant to be healed in God's arms, but Luke was meant to be healed here."

Those are the types of signs God wants us to see. Signs that he built for us with his own hands, moving people into positions beyond their comfort zones, stretching the depths of our relationships with each other and realizing our interdependence as a people. We value the pursuit of freedom so much, perhaps above all else. But I wonder if in this dizzying chase to escape the constraint of being affected beyond our control by circumstances and people, have we lost our sense of belonging to something that is bigger than ourselves? Being a part of something that on the one hand may shrink our view of individualism, but on the other hand liberates us to a new kind of freedom. Freedom from ourselves. Freedom from the maddening quest for control. In all my seesawing back and forth between good "signs" and bad, trying to control their meaning and manipulate their outcome, there wasn't an ounce of freedom to be had. It was just another form of control. One that left me enslaved. It took something as heinous as childhood cancer to show me that our own mind can also be our biggest ball and chain. Fear - a massive iron ball attached to the battered chain-links of our own limited understanding. In the constant pull of life, we attempt to drag it from one place to another, under the delusion that if we drag it successfully to the next phase, we are then masters of our own domain. We stand there triumphant with our hands raised, but our feet shackled.

This is not triumph. This is tragedy. The kind that Greek playwrights wrote about in centuries past. I thought cancer was the tragedy, but it's not. The way we approach life so driven by fears and worries, so bound to the iron-clad grip of control, this is tragic. But it is not the final chapter! Not for me, and not for Sadie. Surrender is. Whether in death or in life, it is in this moment of surrender that God takes the iron ball from us and gives us a rest from our labor. But we must be ready to let it go. We have to get to the end of ourselves. This is what my son's cancer did to me. It brought me to the place where I couldn't confine all my insecurities into a tight ball and carry them anymore. I couldn't pretend I had it all together, hoping the cracks in my confidence wouldn't surface. I thought by dragging my insecurities behind me I had them confined and under control, but I realize now they were confining me. And the wild part of all of this is that it was through cancer that God revealed a path of freedom. If only we can cut the chains of control...and let it go.

Don't you find it odd, this desire for God to be in control, and yet refusal to give over the reigns? Do you see it in your own life? Think about what you fear the most, and how you spend valuable moments of your life guarding against it. Those fears in the deepest recesses of our minds, controlling so much of our thoughts and actions. What is it for you? Loss...abandonment...rejection...worry about your children or loved ones...fear of failure? What triggers that place you don't want anyone else to see? That place that panics in the night and cries out, "I am afraid!" Sit in that place for a minute. Dare to be uncomfortable for just long enough that you buckle. This is the place we come to just before tasting the sweetness of surrender.

# Chapter 6

Sweet Surrender,
pt.2: can I *really* let go?

So how do you do it? When you have reached the end of yourself, how do you release the ol' ball and chain? Especially when you're afraid to let it all go? As I mentioned before, my sweet surrender came a good year and half after Luke was diagnosed. Two realizations surfaced that enabled me to embrace it. The first was that I was growing to despise my old method of survival. That is what the quest for control is really. A means of surviving. One that we learn at a young age. It protects us for a while, until it turns on us, and begins to control us. With Luke sick, I got to the place where I literally couldn't take it anymore - the seesawing back and forth, the quest for knowing what will be. I had to arrive at the place where I could say, "I don't need, nor do I want, to know what is going to happen or what might happen. I want to live now. And right now I have my son." Living for today - this was a huge step forward.

There is a famous story in scripture about Jesus healing a blind man named Bartimaeus who is begging on the side of the road. Many pastors have preached on the healing aspects of the story, or the theological implications of Jesus giving us eyes to see God, or even the response of following Jesus once we've encountered his healing hand. But there is another great little jewel buried in this story that doesn't get much attention, if at all. It involves Bartimaeus' cloak. The reference in Mark 10:50 notes that when he had an opportunity to encounter Jesus, Bartimaeus threw off his cloak. This "throwing off" can also be translated as a tossing away, or tossing aside, of the cloak. The point here is that this was not a moment of undress but a tossing away of something that was either on or near him that he no longer needed. In the original language of the scripture, as it was first written, it can literally refer to someone taking something off, or tossing it away, because it is now rejected as "undesirable or substandard" (BDAG, 107). In essence it has become unnecessary. Why would the writer of this scripture take such care to offer this detail? It doesn't seem like an important point to make in the story, at least at first glance. But what was a cloak to a beggar? Why was it so necessary to him at one time, but now, after encountering Jesus, so dispensable? The answer lies in the context of a first century blind beggar's plight. There was no infrastructure to provide for his material needs, no office of social services to secure his aid. His livelihood depended on begging on the side of the road where travelers would most often pass by. Now as a *blind* man, he wouldn't be able to see where the coins were being tossed. So out of necessity he would lay out his cloak on the ground for people to throw the coins in as they passed. Then at the end of the day he could wrap up the cloak and securely collect all the coins that were given to him.

See, when Bartimaeus tosses his cloak aside and finds healing from Jesus, it doesn't mean he was hot and didn't want to carry the garment around anymore. It means he was giving up his old means of survival! He was discarding the way he learned to live and function in the world, deeming it now as unnecessary, in exchange for a new way of interacting and sustaining life.

In many respects, this is the challenge of letting go of our own chains and shackles. Without even realizing it, we wear them draped around our body, taking them everywhere! Like a security blanket wrapped safely around us, it is so easy to become attached to our old means of survival - even as they are linked to our own dysfunction! As the outer stitching of the garments fade away, they reveal their true iron clad nature, paralyzing us in a cycle of fear and hurt that never allow us to move forward. We touched on this idea earlier, but it really deserves a closer look. Our "problems" - anxiety, depression, addiction, jealousy, anger, negativity, self-destructive behavior (feel free to fill in your own here) - have in many ways provided a short-term solution to dealing with life. They have become our survival instincts. Consider this for a moment. Our fears of failure keep us from being fully invested (relationally or professionally), or in the opposite extreme cause us to blindly pursue success at the expense of all else. Our insecurities prevent us from daring to reach out for fear of the unknown. Depression cocoons us from the risks of further hurt. Anxiety tries so diligently to keep us from being blindsided. Buried in the pangs of addiction are desperate pleas to numb pain. Behind our jealousies exist futile attempts to control others, hoping they won't leave us, only to find our efforts were in vain and the very catalyst for pushing them out the door. How fast our inferiorities become tools to manipulate those we feel threatened by! How quickly our feelings of inadequacy become convenient reasons to retreat when effort and risk are the requirements for reward! We could go on and on, but in the end it's still all about CONTROL. Risk management. Loss prevention.

In many cases, far more than we may realize, we don't experience the change we profess to desire because deep down we don't really want change. Every one of our "dysfunctions" has given us a temporary remedy for surviving the immediate fear of pain, rejection and loss. And they've usually been acquired at a young age. That's why they're so hard to migrate from. Our dysfunction, in essence, is filling our needs. Needs that lie in the shadows of a life so fragile, so delicate, so filled with uncertainty. Needs that lie crouching in the backdrop of hurts that are so present in suffering, so burned from rejection, so stung in loss. All of this - so cautiously prepared for.

For this reason alone, it can be very hard to find the courage and know-how to toss away our old ways of dealing with life. And yet before we can get up and follow any *new* path God's hand is directing us toward, we have to be willing to first let go of the old ways we've learned to emotionally survive. In these moments we find ourselves stuck. Again, it may be anxiety or prolonged grief, a fight or flight instinct in confrontation, or escape in substances to numb pain. Whatever it is, it is there because it has provided for a need deep within us. And then it turns on us. Before long it begins to own us. With seeming scorn it begins to redefine us, replacing our identities with new untamed characteristics. Shackles appear each day with a new link and a tighter grip. We want to break free, but for so long this has been our safe-haven. With the same hand we use to try and push away the chains that bind us, we grab for them and hold them close, as if they provide our deepest means of security. But if our hands are so busy in this push and pull of life's binding irony, how then can we reach for God's hand?

The answer lies in the same place it did for Bartimaeus. Trust. The sweetness of surrender is found in trusting the hand of God more than the "cloak" we hold in our own. Then we will be free to reach for God's hand. It is a hard task, perhaps one of life's truly great battles. I am thankful that in the times I haven't been strong enough to free myself from the garments that have so tied and bound me, God reached his hand a littler closer and grabbed me. He didn't always untie me from my fetters, no this is a process we must work out with God together, that we might realize and bask in its victory together. There are lessons of strength that he wants us to learn along the way. Instead he grabbed me - cloak, chains and all - and kept me from crumbling.

But while calamity may have been averted, the tragedy of being tied up by your own garment still awaited its release. And so we are back again to the simple issue of trust. Do we trust the cloak, in its comfortable discomfort, or have we reached the end of ourselves and our ways enough to completely trust God in *anything*? No matter what comes? One way or another, we must believe that God has a plan for our life that cannot be derailed by the weapons of misfortune. In the end, we will rise above anything life brings at us because God's hand is the one that lifts us to higher ground as we embrace it. Otherwise we are mere captains standing at the helm with no rudder attached. Just the facade of control we use to pacify ourselves enough to sleep through life's perilous jetties, until we are struck by them. The answer to sweet surrender is trust.

Now, when I say trust, I don't mean a mere calling out to God in the hope that he will become our new method of numbing ourselves. He is not a cloak to be worn. Without realizing it, we can often use God as a means of disconnecting from the reality of this world, even as we hope for the next. No, when I say trust and reach, I mean trusting in a way that causes us to rise up passionately and beckons us to throw away life's wartorn cloak! I mean reaching for his hand because we are inspired to get up and truly live - even if it means in the face of suffering! That's what Jesus did for Bartimaeus. He caused him to believe and trust in God's hand more than he trusted his old way of surviving. That is the place we must also come to - to trust the hand of God more than we have come to trust the shackles on our feet. And I mean this without exception! This is the part that may be hard for some to understand, but, for me, I am completely aware that I needed to get to the place where trust meant, "even if my son passes away." As horrifying as that sounds, the see-sawing between fear and faith, hurt and hope, becomes so exasperating that you have no choice but to release the realm of possibilities and say, "My life will still be found in you God. You will get me through anything that comes to pass." I think this is what people mean when they say, "Give it over to God." This is the only way you'll ever live for today! And like I said, in this fragile world that houses life, today I have my son. Today is a day of life!

So many times I have heard people ask, "But how on earth does one do that? I mean how do you really give it over to God?" Fair enough question. You can't literally take this heavy emotion and place it in God's hands on the couch next to you, right? So what does that look like? The problem lies with the word "give". I am not sure *we* are actually doing anything other than having faith that redemption will somehow follow any suffering we may encounter. It is the most basic of all theology in my Christian faith - there is no empty tomb without first the cross of suffering. So, in faith, we are not really giving it over to God as much as we are removing obstacles that prevent us from receiving his hand of redemption, whatever that may look like. In my life, it has been far more the experience of God taking my burden than it was me having the strength to give it to him. "Give" is an intangible word for someone who is at the point of exasperation. The weight is far too heavy to lift. That's why I prefer the word surrender. We are faced with these life-changing moments, arising even from hurt, where it becomes our chance to toss *our* cloak. To trust in God when life doesn't make sense. To come to the point where you sit with what is, and hope in God even when you feel like you are being slain. And then, by a seeming miracle, God takes this burden and lifts it, even as he unhinges the shackles from your feet and calls you to something new. As I've said already, I just had to get to the end of *myself* first. It wasn't even a choice really. It was either get to that point...or come completely unglued.

When I was first in the hospital with Luke, someone wrote me a letter encouraging me to trust God in all of this. In the letter, he also wrote, "You don't know, God may take Luke, but you still must hold to your faith." Now at the time, when I was still grasping for signs and clues, wanting to hear nothing but positive words, this hit me like a brick in the chest. And frankly, I don't recommend saying this to people when they are fresh out of the gate with their child's illness. But as I look back now, he was right. Getting to the place where hoping and trusting in God was no longer limited or defined by whether or not my son would be healed of cancer was a freeing moment in my life. A victorious moment. It is the understanding that "I am going to be alright, my family is going to be alright, even my son is going to ultimately be alright - in this world or the next - because God is the God of redemption." My hope is beyond this world because it lies in a God who is beyond this world. It is the same hope Sadie relishes in when she thinks of Eva. Salvation is not limited to this disease, my joy is not defined by this moment, and the hand of God is bigger than I realized! And in this,

I was able to smile. The kind of smile that comes from a joy that transcends circumstance.

This leads me to the second realization that allowed me to find the beauty of sweet surrender. The first was growing to despise my old "obsessive compulsive, control seeking, try and piece together perfection" cloak of survival. The second is this - trust in all circumstances breeds a joy that transcends all circumstances. This is what the "I have now, and now I have my son" realization led to…joy. An "I trust life will be okay no matter what happens because in this life or the next, you are the God of redemption" type of joy that awakens something profoundly spiritual within you. It's difficult to explain really. I guess some call it inner peace. Others say a peace that passes all understanding. Either way, peace is certainly the defining characteristic.

Peace is a breeding ground for joy. A feeling like the war is over that wells up within and begins to define you over and above the suffering and struggle. And when peace is within, it breeds a joy that can no longer be taken away from you, because it's not dependent on the externals. It's completely different from happiness, which can come and go with each situation. Trusting that God's hand will right all wrongs enables you to find contentment that doesn't make an ounce of worldly sense given the situation lying in front of you. Trusting in God's hand, over and above my own, in such a way that even death can't shake it, has led to a joy that comes from the new found freedom of living in the moment that is right before me, in good times and bad. Some theologians call this *living in the eternal now*. To me it's just a fancy way of saying there is a joy that comes from an eternal God, and when we bask in it, we bask in him. It reminds me of the people during my chaplaincy, who, as they watched their loved ones passing, reached their hand out to mine and had the courage to smile. As if they knew, this is not the final chapter…something transcends this. And for a moment, they were in it, connected to that "something". The eternal now.

In the Old Testament book of Habakkuk, there lies one of my favorite verses in all of scripture. Habakkuk foresees the coming tragedy and destruction that is going to befall his people, and after lamenting it for a while, comes to the realization that joy is still attainable. Joy transcends circumstance when it is rooted in a God who is beyond our circumstance. It is always there for us if we have the willingness to reach for it. Again, it's different than happiness. Different than casual and carefree laughter. It's a joy that when you come right down to it, doesn't really make sense through the lens of this life…as if it's tied to another.

> Though the fig tree should not blossom, nor fruit be on the vines, the produce of the olive fail and the fields yield no food, the flock be cut off from the fold and there be no herd in the stalls, yet I will rejoice in the LORD; I will *take* joy in the God of my salvation.
>
> Habakkuk 3:17-18, ESV
> (italics added for emphasis)

Lying in God's open hand is a gift for us. It is the gift of joy there for the taking. A joy so deep that it cannot be stolen from us. No situation, cancer, friend or foe can snatch it from us because the hand of God embeds it in our soul.  That place is untouchable by the world and its chariots.  It is a piece of heaven here on earth.  And it allows us to live for today, and find beauty in moments that seem so dark and cloudy.  A ray of the noonday sun that peeks in to remind us of the light that is beyond any cloud hovering above us.  It is always there, even if you can't see it.  A joy that refuses to be defined by our shortcomings, our dysfunctions, or our life's entanglements.  A joy that is perfect amidst a mass of imperfection.  God has been trying to teach me this since I was a just a boy.  But it was through watching my own boy that I would finally come to understand it.  It was there, buried in the lyrics Luke wrote in his song, a sweet surrender that had up until now escaped me.

Read the scripture from Habakkuk again.  Then read Luke's song again.  There's something in there for us.  Something we've been waiting to uncover.  This is sweet surrender.  The place the hand of God brings us to that allows us to stop worrying about tomorrow and live for the beauty of today.  Sure, it's easier if you aren't the one sick.  But how could I help Luke find his joy in suffering if deep down I didn't think there was any to be found?  From here, everything changed.  Not because the circumstances changed, but because I changed.  Did I still have my tearful mornings from time to time with God?  Of course!  But his empowering hands lifted me from that place and strengthened me to reach out my hands, and pick my son up, throw him over my shoulder and *carry* him through our back yard - "Lukey, there are 50,000 people looking on, we are heading for the goal line...touchdown!"  And from there we found laughter together.  We found it playing bowling in hospital rooms (our apologies to the night staff at Baystate!), riding wheelies in wheelchairs, and having deep talks at night listening to old Beatles records. I no longer needed future plans of taking this family somewhere. We were already there.

This place is there waiting for you to notice it. And if you're blind to it for too long, the hand of God will make it appear in ways you can no longer ignore. A place where your fears no longer control you, because they no longer cause you to want control. You were destined to reach this place. In the strangest of moments, it appears right before you. A crossroads where change suddenly seems possible and life has hope because of it. Grab this moment! Throw caution to the wind and embrace it! Today, *you* are alive.

# Chapter 7
## Deaf Ears For an Old Voice

No matter how much we have come to believe in joy in all circumstances, there is still a guilt-ridden reaction that creeps back in when you're having fun during your child's cancer treatments. Joy stems from an inner peace and contentment in all things, but fun and happiness while your child is sick can seem at times like a guilty pleasure. Like we are trivializing the plight. I think anyone who has walked a loved one through a time of suffering understands this. It's as if there's a voice saying, "How can you have fun while he's hurting and the stakes are so high? How dare you?" I heard this voice the loudest during our Make-A-Wish trip to Orlando at Give Kids The World. We had an amazing time visiting Disney, Universal, Sea World and Gatorland - all without waiting in any lines (if you can imagine that)! There are perks to being the family of a sick child. Many people want to reach out their hand to help. I watched people wait over an hour for one ride on Space Mountain and our family rode it three times in 20 minutes. The staff at Give Kids the World was amazing, and they pretty much insisted that we have ice cream for breakfast at least once during our stay.

Perhaps the most touching memory I have is the group of retired senior citizens who volunteered every mealtime to wait on our family. They refused to let us carry our own tray of food or get up for soda refills. They wanted to do everything for us. These were people who were in the so called Golden Years of life, who have worked hard, raised children of their own, and are supposed to finally be given the freedom to be a little selfish now. And all they wanted to do was get us to smile. We were strangers, yet they welcomed us in and made us feel like we were special. They made my son feel like he was a king and not a victim of the plague. Isn't it odd that we can go through our lives, jobs, and families, rarely thinking about the condition someone else is in? Rarely taking the time to smile and make others feel great about themselves in this world? Life is hard enough on us all, and yet we compile its frustrated state with words and actions of disregard.

I remember coming back from this trip, back to pastoral life, watching people struggle to be kind in their marriages, argue over the triviality of minute details, and quarrel over the coldness they breathed on each other. I saw it in myself too. And then I got thinking about what it should mean to be the church. We should be a people that smile and serve each other for the joy of it all. A people who are the first to get up and refill each other's cup with encouragement, knowing that every day is a gift and every year golden, no matter what age. I thought about Jesus words, "As you have done it to the least of these brothers of mine, you have done it to me." The church is supposed to be Give Each Other The World. God's world. But we pass the opportunity by with each neglected hand and each forgone smile. Not all of us. Not all the time. But far more often than should be I think.

It's not like our church is unloving, quite the opposite actually. It's just that we are made up of very real people. People who struggle with the same issues as everyone else, the same enslavement to ego, the same addictions to the self. But we know it! At least we should! And our hope begins to be realized as the hand of God shapes and changes us. Learning to be receptive to that process is at the core of what it means to be the church. What a lesson Give Kids the World offers us in this regard! Sacrificial love for your neighbor... and even for a family of strangers, who have become your neighbor simply because your heart has taken up residence alongside them.

Truly, it was a trip that couldn't be replicated again. Each day was there for the taking. But in passing moments of strained calm, in times of crowded solitude where my mind was alone in a sea of people, I sunk back to ask "the questions". Is it right that we should profit from my son's condition? Is this ocean of kindness even reality, or a reminder that we have entered another world? A world whose kindness is its oddity. How strange it will be to return, and what's worse, would we want to?

People will read this and say out of instinct, "of course your son deserves to have fun after all he was going through!" And again, they'd be right. But what about the times that the trip became selfish for us as a family...for me personally? It may have only been staggered moments here or there, but after the kids picked the 8th ride they wanted to go on, Nikki and I put in a "we want a turn" plea. Was that fair? After all, we were all hurting, and all needed a respite of fun from the heaviness of life. Was this trip for Luke only, to comfort his condition, or for a family that was hurting? Of course, it's both. Primarily for Luke, but also a gift for the whole family to find healing in. They tell you that from the beginning in the Make-A-Wish interview process. But while some kids pick the "meet your favorite celebrity", Luke chose Give Kids The World. As parents we certainly encouraged this decision. We thought of building a memory for our family that would last a lifetime. We showed Luke pictures of Disney and Universal's new Harry Potter ride, which we knew would propel him to exclaim "Orlando!" instead of "Paul McCartney & Ringo Starr!" (and yes my son, a Beatles fan like his dad, was weighing those two options). Let it be said for the record, I would have loved to meet the surviving Beatles! But knowing this was a trip we couldn't afford on our own for the family, with a chance to do it skipping the long lines, we certainly built up the excitement. In reality, we were showing him his possibilities that we thought he would really be excited about. But that nagging voice kept asking, "Why are you gaining something from Luke's pain?"

I hated that voice. I hated it whenever it showed

up. The owner of that voice followed me wherever I went. He came uninvited on the Harry Potter ride, sat next to me during the dolphin show at Sea World, and whispered to me at night in our Give Kids the World villa. If the man with that voice would just disappear and leave us to enjoy the moment we had been given. But his voice was so familiar, I was sure I had heard him long before Make-A-Wish...long before cancer... long before I even had kids. He always questioned everything I did, asking me my true motives, checking for cracks in the picture perfect landscape before me. I know this voice all too well. And once again I was asking myself, "Are you going to have fun in this mess of imperfection?"

When I was in my late twenties I remember my father telling me, "Ryan, you were so intense as a child. Everything was so serious and heavy. All I wanted was for you to have fun and be a kid." He was right. That's how life has always been. Overanalyzing instead of enjoying. For some people being obsessive-compulsive dominates their possessions. As mentioned earlier, yes, I struggled with some of that. But by far, mine was a prison of the mind. Thoughts that sought to shatter contentment and replace it with angst and uncertainty. Uncertainty about me and who I truly am. Every dropped pass or missed at bat, a tainted mark on a legacy that no one knew of, or cared of, except me in my own idealistic world blanketed with the masochistic facade of perfection. Vanity of vanities.

Now, as God would have it, I was faced with that nagging reality again. This time involving my child. Would it take this moment from me...from us as a family? Would I struggle through the struggle, or choose joy in it? And then it came. Another moment sprouting from the seedbed of sweet surrender. I threw caution to the wind and enjoyed every moment I could possibly muster with my family on that trip. The voice inside that nagged me could no longer overpower my children's smiles as they fed the dolphins and raced to the next adventure ride. We screamed on Space Mountain and twirled with Harry Potter. We had ice cream for breakfast and loved every minute of it. The pestering voice of insurrection was there, but it began to fall on deaf ears. It was no longer my voice, because I was no longer owning it. We were going to have fun in this mess.

It really comes down to the lesson I tried to teach myself many years ago, when I scratched a rock on my truck and drove off with a smile - things can be just perfect when they just aren't perfect. Motives and emotions become swirled up in a tornado of competing voices, all vying for attention as they race from your mind to your mouth. But which voice we choose to listen to is just that - a choice. A choice ultimately between fear and contentment. Can fun exist when its tenets are beyond our control? Can we lower our guard enough to slide through the mud of life's playground? If we are brave enough to live with contentment! What a courageous undertaking when the costs are so high and the fragility of life shadows in the background of each day's landscape. What joy is ours when we dare to live in the face of life's complexities!

Now, for all the hard time I give myself about overthinking things, I will say my vices have certain virtues associated with them (at least potentially). Overthinking it may be, but I was going to do my best to ensure that while we were *a* family having fun in the mess of childhood cancer, we didn't become *the* family who is defined by it. Suffering, like our dysfunctions, threatens a mutiny of our identity. A cloak worn with the constant expectation of rain. If we grow too used to it, people will start to recognize us only when it is draped across our shoulders. Without knowing it, we can begin to reach for it out of instinct, almost eager to put it on. It becomes strangely comfortable in the familiarity of heartache. There comes a point where your suffering begins to be engrained into personality, and a new identity surfaces from the pains of this rebirth. So forming is the wake of tragedy. So safe the cold embrace of suffering can be when we warm to it. It may be overkill at times, but I think one of the major tragedies of our time is the downright refusal of people to look inward and critically at themselves, and see how often we run to the very state we say we want to overcome. Like a moth to flame, we are drawn by it. So I continually asked of our family, if only silently to myself, "Who have we become, and who are we becoming?" Then, in the tender moments with my son before the day ended, I challenged him (as well as myself) to not let this mutiny of identity become a reality!

This tension of embracing your condition but not letting it define you can best be seen in two contrasting events that happened during our son's treatment. The first was during our Make-A-Wish trip. While at the Hard Rock Cafe someone in the booth behind us saw our Make-A-Wish pins and anonymously paid for our meal. We never met them, never had a chance to thank them. My wife and I both had our eyes filled with tears when the waiter told us that our meal had been paid for. Something about seeing children sick brings out the best in humanity. But I remember thinking also, "we have to be careful that these pins don't become our merit badges." In the quest to be a family and not *that* family, there is a fine line between "do I have to tell this story again" and "did I tell you this story yet?"

It was a second event, however, that really smacked me in the face with this tension. This one occurred after our trip to Orlando. In an effort to catch up to my parents driving in a car in front of us (with a good head start), I became a little too heavy on the gas pedal. Before long, the dreaded red and blue lights began flashing behind me. As the state trooper pulled us over my mind raced to the pins of the past. If only he knew what we were going through, he would let us go. If he saw the pins on our chest, he would gladly overlook this. Oh, how those Make-A-Wish pins can represent both pain and possibility. So slippery a slope! So self-indulgent the shame! It was just a thought. I couldn't help myself really. It just...well...popped in there. I didn't act on it. I didn't find a way to sneak our family heartache in there. But that voice came creeping up again, if only for a second! "Are you trying to profit from this Ryan?" Oh, the owner of that voice had followed me again! Still uninvited. I moved my head to see clearer in the rearview mirror, and there he was. Looking right back at me. With just enough profile for me to see him wink as if to say, "I'm still here."

But that voice doesn't dominate like it used to, second guessing my every move. It doesn't replay over and over in my mind, because I am not afraid of it anymore. I don't own it any longer. Its echo may still stir in me every once in a while, but even that just reminds me that ultimately we all find our full healing in a place somewhere beyond this world. And I am ok with that. The delayed gratification would have bothered me years ago. Now, it's just perfect.

Can you picture this world to come? It's closer than you think. There are little glimpses of it all around us, little moments of intersection with this world and the next, as if God is using the present to reveal what is coming. You just have to be open to see it. And unfortunately this world does so much to close us down. But faith and the hand of God open us back up. They allow us to dream again. Let your mind recapture the spirit of imagination…and dream with me a while. Catch the vision of a world and time where all our infirmities, dysfunctions, and struggles will seem like a blink in a never-ending landscape. Until then, maybe it's time we take life a little less serious. To be kids again. Maybe it's time to have fun in this mess.

God, so gracious is the life that let's go of the hands that control us and embraces your hand instead. What peace to have our lives found not in what latches on to us, but in latching on to you. You Give Us the World, and the adventure of a lifetime is all around us. My wish, if I might be so bold to ask, is for us all - that we may find the courage to climb aboard, resist the urge to grab the wheel, and finally learn to embrace the ride!

# Chapter 8

## Hands Waving In the Water

All this pushing and pulling, reaching and retracting, learning to let go and embrace, we learn so much about the way we handle stress and fear in life. We change from it. But the impact of this ongoing movement can cause us to shelve much of the life we knew before. Inevitably, there are people who find themselves sitting on those shelves, waiting to be picked up again, waiting for life to go back to normal. They are unaware of the deep changes that are taking place within us, and, especially with children, may be unable to get their head around the magnitude of the moment. With childhood innocence they may be more inclined to reach out their hand in vulnerability, as life has yet to fill their palms with the links of iron that one day will become their shackles. But unless they see a familiar outstretched hand, how will they reach for it? As we are latching onto God in our moments of unrest, we must remember that there are others who are looking to latch onto us. To them, our hands seem as large as life, strong and secure...almost god-like. Of course, we find out quickly we can't fill God's shoes. And yet there are people who are hurting with you, who may or may not know how to reach out to God for themselves. They are looking for you to lead them. The responsibility is great, especially as you are wrestling through it all yourself. And if you aren't careful, you'll miss them.

We have two hands. At first they are both holding on for dear life, but once we are confident and secure holding the hand of God, knowing that he doesn't let go and his palm is large enough to hold us, we must take the other hand and stretch it out. We just might find there is another hand flailing out there, waiting to latch on.

My middle child, Caleb, was always extremely close to his brother, Luke, growing up. As a toddler, he looked up to Luke for everything, as most younger brothers do. Luke was his playmate, his confidant in discovering the great mysteries of the world that exist in the mind of a 5 year old, and his model for navigating around the landmines of adventure that would get him into trouble. If Luke was playing guitar, Caleb was playing guitar. If Luke was fishing off the staircase of the house for undiscovered species of imaginary fish, Caleb was fishing off the staircase with him. It's the kind of relationship I never had growing up as the only boy, but always wanted.

When Luke got sick, Caleb, already a more reserved child with his feelings, became even more emotionally withdrawn. His hospital visits were quiet and confusing. I could see the internal conflict that was warring in him. Part of him wanted to do what Luke was doing, because that is what Caleb always did. There may have even been an innocent envy of the attention Luke was getting, which came out when people brought Luke gifts and Caleb asked with teary eyes, "what about my presents?" When I reasoned with him about why we give presents to kids in the hospital, his first response was, "I wish I could be in the hospital too!" Of course he would. That's where his brother was. That's where the adventure of the day was lying dormant waiting to be discovered.

But then there were the moments of confusion. His brother didn't look the same. His mouth was covered with a mask, his body connected to tubes and machines that he carted around. Every few hours Luke would leave with one of us and come back looking deflated. That look. When someone reaches a point where all their blood counts are low and life is a struggle to get up and move, their body skinny from a lack of desire to eat, their face gaunt and pale - there is just a look about them that chills the eye with the reality of death. It had to have been hard on Caleb. I'm sure the mixed emotions of seeing Luke getting a lot of attention and gifts, living an adventure without him, coupled with an image of his brother that was...well, not his brother, was a heavy load for a 5 year old to carry around. And I really should just admit, he was being overlooked. Both Caleb and our youngest boy, Eli, were being overshadowed. It wasn't intentional. It was survival. But it had to change.

Eventually, I tried to have a father-son heart to heart with the other boys about Luke, and how they were processing it all. Eli, whose open heart is his biggest strength, shared his encounter with cancer as both an onlooker and as one affected by its tentacles as it metastasized into the life of our family. He spoke of sadness and hope in his own way, with his own words, and was not too ashamed to cry. I guess he's just strong that way. But Caleb was removed. He brushed by the topic as if he was determined to get somewhere else in his mind, like a man speed-walking the streets of the big city desperate to get to a place he may never reach, oblivious to the life happening all around him. He may have said that he was sad, but it was the kind of response that was more a regurgitation of what he knew he was supposed to say. He shrugged his shoulders and looked to the left to refocus on that other place he needed to get to. It was a response that came from a distant place, far off in the horizon of a heart that fears pain more than the rest of the body does.

Caleb has a unique threshold for pain. Physical pain. Friends of ours would laugh at how rugged he is. I can still remember the look on people's faces after he ran head first into a wood beam from a raised deck, legs out from under him, and then got up with immediate egg on his forehead and said, "Wow, I didn't see that one at all!" But when it comes to emotions, well...that's another story. He protects himself with a cocoon that never unravels to allow him the freedom to fly. We knew he must be hurting. He must have. But getting him to talk about it was like drawing water from a stone. We wouldn't have even heard of his pain at all until a flashback he had triggered it two and half years later.

We were visiting Nikki's father in a rehabilitation hospital after a serious burn accident. The boys were there to see their Pépé and give him some encouragement on the road to recovery. At this point, he didn't look burned anymore, with the exception of his legs, which were tightly bandaged and covered. All the boys ran in to see him except for Caleb who hung back by the door. What he was experiencing didn't really hit me at first, and I said, "Caleb, go say hi to your grandfather. Give him a hug." But he didn't want to. Nikki and I just looked at each other with a puzzled and annoyed expression. I guess at first we thought he was being rude. Caleb's shyness has at times come across as rude or indifferent, and we have worked with him on more than one occasion to respond to people with a little more engagement than that man rushing the city streets looking for his unknown destination. Where is he running to as life is hurrying by? Is he running to something or from something? Sometimes the people who seem the most standoffish are really wrestling with the most insecurity. Who or what was Caleb hiding from? His grandfather or something else? What was hiding in that room that caused him to do the same?

I knelt down next to him by the doorway and said, "Caleb, what's up? Why are you being so shy?" Typical of Caleb, he couldn't articulate his feelings and gave the common, "I don't know." But the stare in his eye told me he was in more thought than he was leading on, so I took a chance and said, "Does this remind you of Lukey being in the hospital?" And in a snap, all the emotions that were buried in soil of his heart were dug up. His eyes got teary, and he nodded his head in agreement. "I don't like hospitals," he replied. Here it was. He was hurting...and what's more, he was sharing! I hugged him close and whispered so no one else could hear, "I understand bud, but it's okay now. Pépé will be all right. And your brother Luke is all right now too. You don't have to be afraid anymore." That's all it took. Just a little tapping into the soil to help loosen what had hardened. And then he was free. Before long, he was talking to his grandfather about his injury and sitting on the bed with him. It just took a little awareness on our part. Awareness of the people in the background who may be hurting too, but can't find the platform to voice it *because* they're in the background. Their voice doesn't carry that far. So that's where they stay. Distant and removed. Wondering where their own significance plays into the moments that are unfolding before them.

Think of it like a sinking boat. When life strikes you like a tidal wave, it takes all your strength just to focus on surviving the hit. You can't help but look through a spyglass at the island you must reach together for safety. But when you look through a spyglass you are also oblivious to the surrounding ripples that spread out in the wake of the storm. Those ripples rock other boats too. They have a powerful effect on anyone in their projectile. If the initial wave is big enough, then the resulting wake may be large enough to capsize them as well. We may find that the people closest to us feel like they're drowning with us, floating in a current that's taking them to a place they don't want to go. As they stare at the aftermath of the giant wave that struck, they may be too stunned to ask for help. But that doesn't mean they don't need you. They might be waiting for you to reach your hand out to them, afraid that their additional weight might sink both of you. As you approach them, you might hear the faintest of voices whisper under their breath, "I am drowning here too!"

I heard this whisper when I looked at my father, who had for months since Luke's diagnosis had a distant stare in his eyes that spoke of fear and worry. I could hear its faint echo as he paced back and forth in front of the window of the hospital meeting room where the doctor first told me and Nikki about Luke's diagnosis and treatment plan. You know, the room that always has a box of tissues sitting on the table as you walk in.

If you look and you listen, you'll hear it, "I'm drowning in this wake!" It was in Eli's newly discovered upset tummy that oddly coincided with Luke's chemotherapy treatments. It was layered in my mother's daily phone calls to talk about nothing, other than the need to share her plans for the day and ask if we needed anything.

There are many hands reaching out for God in these moments. As they reach for God, they grab someone else's hand, hoping they just might find God's there too. People heard my voice silently scream, "I'm drowning!" and after a while I heard them echo it back. One day in particular stands out in my mind, where the faint screams that lingered under our breath crossed paths and resonated a new tune of hope. My mother had offered to watch Luke while I went to work. She knew I was stressed so she had Luke call to ask if I'd come home and eat lunch with them. Truthfully, work sometimes took my mind off the constant reminders of Luke's condition, his swollen face and bald head. You don't see your child that way...but you do see *it*. Still, how could I say no? I gave them a time I'd be there, and when it came, I walked through the door expecting to see those "reminders" looking at me again, in case I'd forgotten them. I guess I was just having a bad day.

What I didn't expect to see was a neatly set table in our dining room with a framed card stock that read on one side "Bradley Grille: with menu items by Luke Bradley". On the other side, a list of the specials for the day: grilled cheese, tuna sandwich, tuna melt, hamburger, cheeseburger, French fries, iced tea, soda and water. Luke came up and said, "Welcome to the Bradley Grille, come this way sir and I'll seat you." Then he asked for my order. He wrote it down on a pad and brought it into the kitchen where they began to cook. I could hear them laughing and having fun, but my eyes were fixed on the words "Bradley Grille". I locked eyes on it, and we just stared at each other. Somewhere in that moment, the fears of his future collided with the dreams for his future, and I could do nothing except let my emotions out as quietly as I could, hoping no one would see or hear. But I cherish this memory. It's a memory of rocking up and down in the wake and seeing us all pull together to swim for the boat that would take us to shore. A moment when we climbed in together and rowed, taking turns when one of us got weak and tired. A time when I felt the movement of the boat inch closer to the island destination, and thought not only about our arrival, but about what lay awaiting for us, for Luke, once we settled in.

These are the moments when people reach their hand out to you as you reach your hand out to others. And the fingerprints you leave behind are not just your own. Somehow as you lift up your hand, you realize the prints that remain are far too big to be yours. They are of a hand large enough to hold even the very sea that surrounds you. A hand strong enough to lift you all to safety while teaching the waters the joy of contentment. Yet this hand is also soft...comforting enough to find rest for a tired soul who has reached the end of himself. Yes, these are the precious moments that kings and queens cannot afford, and yet even the most downtrodden receive. Times that carry you as you carry others, if you are courageous enough to be vulnerable and to know that being in need of another is a place of hope and not weakness.

I want to take this opportunity to thank my wife for her strength when we all needed it and for the way she shared this load with such grace. For the first two years, the flexibility of my job allowed me to take Luke to his regular treatments. But I got to the point where I was so drained from it, so emotionally exhausted, I couldn't do it anymore. Luke did not do well with accessing his port - a surgically implanted line that, when accessed by a fairly thick needle, sends the chemotherapy directly into the body's circulation - so every treatment became a nightmare for both of us. Physically for him, emotionally for me. For two years I had to hold him down while he cried. He would yell out the same phrase that broke my heart the first week in the hospital, "Why are you doing this to me?!!" Is there any parent who can't understand just how devastating that is? How it rips your heart from your chest and dashes it to pieces on the ground?

Finally I reached the point, where I couldn't handle it anymore. The last time I took him to treatment, after hearing that scream for the last time, I turned to the window and started sobbing like a baby. I didn't mean to cry in front of Luke. The last thing I wanted was for him to feel worse. It just came out. But an amazing moment also came from it. A voice that had softened from anger to tenderness breathed, "Dad, why are you crying?" I lifted my head up and said with all I could muster, "Because I'd give anything to trade places with you and take this pain so you wouldn't have to." "Why would you want that?" he asked. My response was short and to the point. "Because I love you Luke. Don't you know how much I love you?" That was it. He perked right up. His tears were gone, and he was smiling again. The hurts of the previous moment had been written into the pages of the past. Is there anything more powerful than love?

Love. Not the kind we use to describe our favorite food or sport, but the kind that comes in the form of sacrifice and finds residency in the midst of suffering. This is where God is when it hurts. He's in the same place as a father who wants to trade places with his son, or a wife who takes her husband's burden when he can't hold onto it anymore. In many ways I felt powerless in this journey to do what I knew God could do. I couldn't fix it. I couldn't take Luke's pain from him. But in some ways, I guess I did. I guess we all did. We did it for each other. Not in a way that eliminated suffering altogether, but in the longer moments that followed...redemption came.

I guess that's how God works. He doesn't always remove us from suffering, but he always brings a thread of redemption to it. *Redemption* - this movement of God's hand that heals and restores our soul to a place of victory, triumphant even over the pain it took to get there. A victory that only knows its champion because it has found the strength to overcome. A champion who carries us from the place where we dared to whisper, "I'm drowning!" to the place where the shackles of life's antagonists lay breathless at our feet. Again, it doesn't mean we won't scream like a young child who doesn't understand the reason for his suffering, "Why are you doing this to me?" It just means that like that day in the treatment room, suffering is not the final chapter. Whether in life or in death, suffering is not the climactic end. Not when the story rests in the hands of God. And from it, we will know the victory of what it means to overcome...what it means to really live. We will know what it means to be loved by the God who is love. And in this raging sea, he provides us the chance to truly love each other.

Thank you mom and dad, my sisters Karen and Allison, surrounding family and true friends - for having the courage to hold God's hand on one side, as you reached out to us with the other. We were all flailing for a bit, weren't we? But you grabbed our hands and put it in God's. He used you, and we got the privilege to see it. You supported us as we all supported Luke. Thank you. For three and a half years we rowed this boat together, pressing against the waves to reach our island destination that seemed so far off in the horizon. And then, before we knew it, we were there. It was over. Luke, you made it!

# Chapter 9

## Anywhere But Normal

It was the beginning of spring. Everything around us was testifying to the newness of life. Luke was weeks away from his final treatment and I should have been on the top of the world, moving from fear of the striking waves to surfing the last one home. We were all excited, and I was too, for the most part. But there was another part of me that felt confused, maybe even a fear something was going to pass away. How strange is that? My son beat cancer, and I'm worried about something dying. It wasn't about Luke. I was literally ecstatic for him. It was me. I had learned so much and grown so accustomed to holding onto God's hand for dear life over the last three years. What happens now? Does the end of this journey mean releasing my hands to be free to my own vices again? But I grew so comfortable resting there...in the hands of God. I had moments so rich in experiencing God in those tender mornings and late evenings, when no one else was around. I was free to pour myself out to him - my fears and guilts, gratitudes and joys. I couldn't possibly think of going back to "normal". What does that even mean? Would I rely on God everyday with the same intensity? Or go back to a life filled with a false sense of security, waiting for the iron ball and chain to hitch themselves once again to my ankles...until the next wave struck?

The reality of this question hit me hard one day when someone asked me, "Are you ready for things to go back to normal again?" That question whacked me in the head so powerfully it could have flipped me. I was driving in my car and began to come to tears, in a way that only compared to the tears shed when Luke was first diagnosed. I remember looking up to God and yelling out, "What is normal?!" Does it mean going about a carefree day again with the naivety I had before all this started? Can you ever really go back to that place again? Does it mean that God heads to the backdrop of everyday life, as I seek to be the lord of my landscape yet again? Oh, no, I can't go back there! I know too much now. Life is as precious as it is fragile. We spent three years rowing for the shore with such vigor that we dared not look left, right or behind, for fear of the coming waves. Now we were supposed to set our oars across the bow of the boat and coast in. For the first time in a long time, I looked around. The seas were calm, but I was still afraid of being blindsided by a rogue wave. And again I cried out as I drove, "What does it mean to be normal, God? How do you want me to live?"

What a strange concept...normalcy. I wonder if any of us are really normal at all. What's worse, I now believe the way we define normal is not really as it was intended to be anyway. And so we build our walls, wear our masks, and carry our ball and chain from one spot to the next. I don't know that I could ever go back to the way life was before cancer hit our family. But what's more, I can honestly say I wouldn't want to. Do I wish my son didn't have to go through it, of course! But I wouldn't go back now. I am all too happy to have my definition of normal replaced. It was rolled into an ideal of perfection that was far too abnormal to be real. A butterfly I chased but couldn't catch, only to find that when I finally collapsed in exhaustion, he landed on my shoulder. And as I gazed at him, I realized he wasn't perfect at all. There were scars and spots where his wings had been worn through the wind. He wasn't perfect. He was just beautiful, that's all.

Do you know the joy of an abnormal life with God? A contentment that transcends circumstance and a peace not confined by our situation? I would have taken my son's illness to save him, in an instant. But the truth is, over three years, he took the illness and saved me.

God works in mysterious ways, as the saying goes, which is great if you love mystery, but frustrating if you need all of life to resolve and be accounted for. What has become increasingly obvious as I walk this mystery is that life has cancer. It doesn't always surface as a tumor or become identified in blood counts and radial imaging. It registers in the scans of our eyes as we look around and see the fear of pain, loss and helplessness that people run from each and every day. Back and forth in different directions, on subways and commutes, rushing from one appointment to another, then back to the hospital beds that await us each night in the comfort of our own homes. Disguised with familiar linens and blankets of security, we crawl in and face our moments of solitude, where a voice within reminds us of our battle and analyzes our prognosis based on the results of the day's events. Life has cancer. Turn your gaze inward, scan across the canvas of your life and you will see it in yourself. From this understanding of life and the knowledge of self, what becomes abundantly clear is - there is never a time to let go of the hand of God. Even the thought of going back to "normal" makes me whisper to God all the more, "Don't let go!"

Look and see the cancer that grows all around us. A callousness of deadened cells of the heart, with new ones dying each time we feel jaded from the day. It's in the way we treat each other and the defensive postures we use to hide our insecurities. I watch it in my children, in how they learn to adapt and respond after feeling rejected or demeaned. Something begins to change in them. It happens in all of us. We inevitably learn how to reject and demean others. Some of us learn to use this weapon of defense with more vigilance, depending on how deep the wounds pierced our own skin. This became so clear to me the day I returned to work, right after taking my first week retreat to start this book. Having spent days putting together my thoughts on Luke's cancer and how it affected me, I walked into the church Monday morning to learn of a bunch of issues that surfaced while I was gone. I sat and listened to personality clashes, conflicts of ideas, people reacting out of their own feelings of inferiority, all while claiming Christ as the catalyst of their concern. But I could see just how much people's fears were dominating them, leading them right to their own traps of brokenness. I saw people, who I knew were hurting, walking right into the choices that initially caused them pain to begin with. Drawn to it out of habit and the facade of being in control.

Like I said before, churches are made up of "normal" broken and hurting people, just like me. United initially by our common abnormalities, but then more triumphantly by our common faith to carry us through it. People who struggle, just like I do, to find the courage to throw the cloak of enslavement that is no longer our identity nor our destiny. I think the greater testimony of the church will be found not only in our thoughts about God (which we are often willing to share), but in how we have been, and are being, changed! In my experience, people are far less likely to share those thoughts, because it takes vulnerability and the courage to break down the walls of insecurity.

Look around some more, do you see the cancer in our world? We speak of it only when tragedy strikes - childhood illness, school shootings, war - but these are the outpouring *symptoms* of a deeper rooted illness. They are the bruises and gaunt faces of a struggle within that rages against us and seeks to ravage our spirits. It may not be the legacy that all of us are known for, but we all battle it. Under the surface it defines us more than we realize. Obsessive-Compulsive Disorder - a mutated cell that feeds as it grows into a life of its own, dominating the healthy cells that once thrived. Anxiety and depression - the identifying blood counts of the fear, guilt, and helplessness that ravages the human soul. Anger and addictions - the scanned images of deep seeded pain and worthlessness that traps and binds us. Isolation - the fatigue of rejection that knows no comfort. Find out what *owns* you, and you will find your cancer. Feeding and filling, growing and suffocating as it wraps around the most vital parts of the body. To remove it now is dangerous. Can we survive without it?

This is where the hand of God must touch and heal us - right in the very place that we are being owned. That's where we need to be set free! Luke may have survived cancer medically, but his greater fights will come in the days ahead when he faces these other forms of cancer within. Will he persevere with the same determination I saw in him over these last three years? I have to believe he is more equipped now than most of us ever are. I can already see it - a refusal to be defined by any ailment (emotionally or physically) or owned by any dysfunction. But the struggle is there. Chemotherapy greeted him when he was tall and fast, and then excused him shorter and slower. His wish when his treatments ended was to grow. He doesn't like being one of the smallest in his class, nor does he like the fact that his younger brother is now faster. So what does he do? Does he withdraw and hide in the shadows of fear and insecurity? Inferiority and inadequacy? No... he picks football for his first sport back in action. My pride doesn't come from hearing, "Luke is at the 30...the

20...the 10...touchdown!" like I once recited with him in the backyard. It comes from his coach who came up to me and said, "I love that your son isn't afraid out there. He'll go against a bigger kid in a hitting drill just to make a statement." He may be one of the smallest kids on the squad, but in many ways he's stronger than I ever was. He is learning, at a young age, how to confront those giants of fear out there.

Normal? I think I'll pass on it. Frankly, it sounds a little boring to me now. Scary actually. God's hand holds something far more extraordinary in it for us. It's called Life. Not defined by length or circumstance, but by that intersection point where the tips of our fingers begin to feel God's. It grows from there to a place of embrace, where insecurity turns secure, inferiority changes to worth, and inadequacy becomes confidence. Remember that famous painting, The Creation of Adam, by Michelangelo? It depicts so accurately what has become a normal life for so many of us. God's hand and ours are so close...our fingertips almost touching...but just falling short. Even Adam's reach is so half-hearted...so expecting to miss. The nonchalant extension of someone who has grown used to feeling that, as nice of a concept as God is, ultimately we are on our own. Unfortunately, I guess that's normal. I suppose that's why sadness and fear crept in the moment someone asked me if I was ready to return to it.

Normal? Who needs it? I'm content right where I'm at. Finally. And the blessing of an abnormal life with God, if you don't already know it, is there for the taking. It doesn't always make sense. Sometimes it even feels like hell. But have faith...it's just God walking you through the desert sands. That's the way to the land of promise. I'd say this was an unfortunate detour, but there are just so many "out of the norm" lessons to be learned along the way. Lessons that will make the fruit of fertile ground taste all the sweeter.

# Chapter 10

## The Wasteland Isn't Wasted Land

What lessons have I learned in all of this? That's a question that inevitably follows struggle of any kind. By now, my answers are probably clear. They've been highlighted features throughout this book: chaos and beauty can share the same space, life can be just perfect when it just isn't perfect (if we dare to stay present in it), the desire to control stems from fear and ends up controlling us, our dysfunctions have in many ways been our closest companions (our cloaks), the ability to let go and trust in all circumstances liberates us to joy that transcends circumstance, there is cancer all around us in many forms, and above all...there is never a time to let go of God's hand! Whew! Is that all of them? Nope. I forgot - my wife is stronger than me. So is my son for that matter. He's stronger than both of us!

But there is still a lesson about the *character* of God

that was revealed in this journey. Something about the nature of who God is that has been illuminated in the path of suffering and gives me the newly found desire to hold the hand of God in all the other areas of my life. It's really the overarching umbrella from which all the other lessons find their merit. We've hinted at it already. It's coming to know God as The Redeemer. Not just reading about redemption in the pages of scripture, but encountering the one whose hand parts the seas of life's fiercest battles. The one who turns the tears of brokenness into tears of joy. Redemption comes at different times, and in different forms, but always from the hand of God. For some, it's the love of a newborn child who calms the heartache of loss. For others, it's the experience of God's healing touch. And then there are those whose healing awaits fulfillment in a day still to come, and yet have already found the miracle of joy as they wait for their hope to be realized. All of these people have encountered The Redeemer, and though they may have lost something or someone, many will tell you they've also come away having gained from the experience. Gained an encounter with God that many have never tasted, for many have not allowed themselves the opportunity to be desperate.

The very impulse to ask the question "what lessons have you learned?" reflects an inner longing we all have to see things redeemed. It's a favorite theme in movies, books, and stories we tell around the dinner table. We all know suffering is a reality, but I suspect we aren't all sure that redemption lies on the other side of it. Instead we wait in suspense for how the story of our lives will ultimately end. None of us want our hurts or sufferings, shortcomings or dysfunctions, pains or struggles to become our swan song. Surely there has to be a final chapter that closes out the saga of our lives. Will it be liberation from *Shawshank* or the tragedy of *Hamlet*?

The word *redeem* can mean many things. All of the following definitions are in Merriam-Webster's online dictionary: "to buy back, to get or win back, to free what distresses or harms, to change for the better, repair, restore, to free from a lien by payment of an amount secured, to offset the bad effect of." How accurately these all describe the work of God! And nowhere more than in the desert heat of suffering. That's where God's hand of redemption meets us. That's where we see God for who he is.

Many know the story of Moses on Mount Sinai, where he received the Ten Commandments from God. At the very least, we may remember the movie with Charlton Heston. While "Sinai" is the commonly used name for this mountain, it is also known in the scriptures as Mount Horeb. In fact, the first reference to Horeb in Exodus 3:1 identifies it as "the mountain of God". Why is this interesting to us when talking about God's redemptive hand in suffering? The answer lies in one of the etymologies associated with the root word for Horeb. It means *wasteland*. This reflects a lot of what I've learned about God over the last three years (and over the last 40 years really). Gods were always thought to live on mountains in the ancient world; that is certainly nothing new. But while men projected their gods on grand mountains like Olympus, the God of scripture says, "I'll meet you in the wasteland! You know, that mountain that no one wants, surrounded by the desert wilderness that has left you hungry and thirsty. When you find yourself there, I'll be there too!"

I found God there. In the wasteland. Not just with Luke. Not just in my own struggles. But as I visited the wasteland others have wandered in, God was found there. While I held a young woman's hand and prayed for her dying husband, as she looked up and asked me, "Who is going to teach my son how to shave?" God was there. In the tenderness of embrace, hearing her recite the 23rd Psalm while I was moved to a tear, God was there planting a seed of hope. Hope that one day even death will be redeemed and suffering will cease as God wipes every tear from our eye. Oh, how we wait for that unknown chapter to be revealed! It scares us even as it draws us. It is a precious hope to be sure, but it is the redemption that I have found *here and now* that encourages and assures me of the hope that is to come. God's hand of redemption reached down, opened its giant palm and handed me the gift of faith unlike any I had ever known. The type of faith that, as it is lived out, becomes part of your being - shaping and coloring everything you see.

I think that's why the cross of Jesus captures me. In all its suffering - the epitome of pain and death - it is the precursor to life anew. The end of the story is not a plank of suffering, but an empty tomb of renewal. And as we learn to die to ourselves, with all those masks and measures of control, the tomb becomes for us a womb. A womb where new life begins its embryonic state until we are mature enough to walk from it victoriously. Crawl from it if we have to! A life resurrected from the ashes of pain, rejection, and loss. Yes, God understands suffering in the human condition, because he took it to himself, made the wasteland his home, and brought the hand of redemption to it! This whole cycle of life and death, that has us running in such constant fear, finds its conclusion buried in the catacombs. But we are no longer there. We've walked out.

About a year ago a friend of mine came up to me and said, "Have you ever found it fascinating that Jesus, even after he raises from the dead, still has the scars? They're like a part of him now, and it's the scars that end up reminding people of who he is. What once was a symbol of suffering became something beautiful." It's true. The scars symbolize something new now. What was ugly has become beautiful. I guess that's as good a definition of *redemption* as there is. Who would have thought that scars could be so endearing? So strangely comforting they must have been and must be even for us today. So reminiscent of days passed, as they point to what lies ahead. Markers of suffering that are now the very scrolls that proclaim victory and testify what it means to overcome. Scars are the trademark of redemption! When I picture the cross, I see Mount Horeb in its background...and God saying, "I love you without boundaries. So here I am in the wasteland with you. Now let's walk out of this tomb together. You are redeemed."

Of all the definitions in Merriam Webster for redemption, "to change for the better" is my favorite. I suppose because it most closely grasps the idea that what was ugly has become beautiful. It so perfectly speaks to what God has done in me over these last three years - as a father, husband, pastor, and friend. I have grown closer to God, to others, and to myself. Walls collapsed and I wasn't so afraid to be exposed anymore. To see myself, in all my shortcomings, and be okay. For as much as I learned about God, I also learned so much about myself. This process has changed me. I look for the beauty in the day far more than I ever did before Luke's diagnosis. I live for the day more than I ever would have allowed myself the freedom to do in years past. It was a change for the better.

Change is a scary word for a lot of people, but for me it symbolizes hope. Hope that where we are is not where we'll always be. And life, because God is the God of redemption, will eventually change for the better! Maybe because my history is one of always trying to obtain perfection, I am just naturally drawn to this definition. But perhaps that desire for things to be better than they are is not all bad either? Maybe God, as he separated it from immediate gratification and my desire to control the outcomes, just had to redeem it.

There is a verse in scripture that can be life changing, should we have the faith to believe it and the courage to make it our own. It states, "And we know that for those who love God *all* things work together for good, for those who are called according to his purpose" (Romans 8:28, ESV, italics added for emphasis). Not some things. All things. Even childhood cancer. Maybe it's easier for me to say that, knowing my son has survived. Fair enough. But this isn't only about Luke's story. I've heard it ring true for others whose struggles had different outcomes. For Sadie, who, a year after watching her daughter pass, stood with me in front of our congregation to make the same declaration - all things work for good for those who love God because God is good! But all things can only work for good if God has the power to redeem it. And that he does! Our role is to be open to receiving it, even if it means letting go of our cloak and trading it in for something new.

For me, a foundation of faith lies in not only believing this verse from Romans to be true, but living it as true. To believe it takes trust. To live it takes surrender. Surrender isn't chiseled out of textbooks or mapped out on dry-erase boards. It's released in the pains of uncertainty. It comes from staring the biggest of fears in the face and saying, "Slay me as you may, still I will hope and trust in God." Where do we get this courage? Where did Paul, the writer of this verse in scripture, get the courage to pen it - having been beaten and imprisoned, with the constant threat of execution that would eventually take his life? I have to believe the answer lies in the words just a few verses before. "For I consider that the sufferings of the present time are not worth comparing with the glory that is to be revealed to us" (Romans 8:18, ESV).

I don't know why God allows certain sufferings to happen. It's beyond my mind's ability to understand. I just know that when it does happen, and it does in spite of our protests, he is the one to hold on to. He is the one you'll need more than ever. I think everyone, at some point, asks the question, "Why does God allow suffering?" Even those who profess disbelief in God often use this question to support their views. "If God exists, why would he let this happen?" This is the single biggest question I hear from people whose faith has been filled with doubt. You've probably asked this question yourself.  Maybe as you watch the news or witness the day, maybe as you wrestle with your own hurts.  I know I've asked it.  It's a fair question to be sure.  Heartache drives us to the place where we cry out, "God where are you!?  Are you someone who even cares!?"  While I haven't found answers to the question of "why," I have found some for the questions of "where" and "who."  As you wrestle through the story of your own "cancer," I encourage you to think through the underlying lesson of this book…a lesson I learned walking with my family in the trials of my son's cancer.  GOD IS THE ONE WHO'LL MEET YOU IN THE WASTELAND.  He is the one who'll spring water from the desert sands, take the mess of imperfection and bring the perfect thread of redemption to it.  He is the one who can turn your suffering to rejoicing.

# Chapter 11

Raise Your Hands!

When is it too early to start celebrating? Are we counting our chickens before they hatch? Those were the questions during the final month of Luke's treatments. I remember the doctor's words, "Luke will be done with treatments, but still has to have his counts checked once a month in case of a recurrence. Then the following year, once every other month." What?? I thought that was it. For three years he has been in remission, isn't it over? Is it too early to relax and breathe? We had a big party planned to celebrate the journey's end. I may not have wanted to go back to "normal," but I definitely wanted this all to be over. Not just his treatments, but all of it. Luke was all set to ring the bell at the children's cancer ward on his final day of chemotherapy, signifying the end of the struggle. Really, it was just signifying his final treatment, but for me that meant the final day of struggle. I guess those two aren't really the same. Life will always have struggles in it. Each day filled with risks and remissions.

Still, for Luke, the pain of it all was ending. Of course there was reason to celebrate! There always is if we look for it. Celebration and suffering, joy and fear, they walk in tandem with each other. We must choose which to live for. Too often we find reasons to be upset or angry. Why don't we put the same effort into celebrating and rejoicing? The reality is, this was a huge milestone Luke reached. An end to a rough three years for all of us, but none more than him. Fear tried to rob me of it. It has a funny way of doing that, doesn't it? It was almost as if I *needed* this fear and worry to creep back in...maybe to feel "normal" again.

As we've noted throughout this story, fear has an unyielding grip on so much of our lives. So much of our emotional preparations, our attempts to avoid being blindsided, cause us to miss the joy and opportunity that lies in front of us. Fearing what might be and in turn missing what's right here. We all do this to some degree. People burned in love, who never quite love the same way again for fear of rejection's scorpion-like sting. People who find in the despair of loneliness a strange comfort, and in spite of protests that they are alone, are the first to shut down, push away, and protect. Those who endure failures, and in a silence too quiet for even their own ears to detect, vow never to put their heart and soul into anything quite the same way again. Or those so buried with regret they can only come to life once their perspective has been altered by substances that make false promises of a night filled with possibility. All cloaks in the rain.

But this was not a time to fear. Nor a time to hide in the rain. This was a time to celebrate! A time to thank God for the work of his hand and bask in the rays of his blessing! This journey has been draped in the narrative of overcoming fear, and far be it from me to turn back in its final hour. God's hand has been a shade in the scorching heat and a blanket in the coldness of winter, and so will it always be. No matter what comes. The mindset of "I have today with my son," that I learned back when the journey was at its hardest, does it ever become obsolete? I have today. And today is a day for rejoicing!

I can't wait to see Luke grow. To watch him approach battles the way he did this one. To see him pick himself up from failure and face himself when he is afraid. I want to cry at his wedding and hold his children in my arms. To dream of what will be and not let fear snatch the beauty of imagination from my mind. Chains of fear be gone, and take your paralysis with you! You are a lame crutch that has dominated too much of my life. I'll trade what *if*, for what *is*. I'll risk hoping in the unknown. Why? Because I can. And if roads veer in directions that don't match my hopes, I'll make new ones and dream new dreams.

It was a time to celebrate, and celebrate we did. We rented a hall, stuffed ourselves until we could eat no more, and danced until the night tucked us in. Every few hours, a wave of gratitude would come over me, and I remembered to say "thank you". There is a forgotten art called celebration. Not the kind that comes from inebriation or numbing ourselves from life. The kind that wells up inside us like a spring and flows out from the deepest parts of our being.  A celebration that is approached with a sober mind and heart freed, so as to fully appreciate the moment and stay connected to its beauty.  It is indeed an art form.  A painting that has come to life and dances before our eyes.  If only we did this more often - for the joy of it.

Truth be told, this is the chapter I felt would be the hardest to write.  Celebration.  Raising our hands in rejoicing.  You'd think the chapters on experiencing pain or witnessing suffering would have been the hardest, but they weren't.  It was this one.  Why?  For starters, I am making the profession to reach for hope and not fear, for the hand of God and not the wheel of control, and this is something I know at times I will fail in.  I know there will be moments, and there have been already, where I will slip back into fear and anxiety.  I will look to control outcomes and fit them into tight spaces on a staircase.  I am not delusional to this reality.  So what of it?  Does that negate all I have learned and prove the lessons within to be a facade?  Not at all!  It means I'm not perfect.  But I remember what I've learned – *maybe that's just perfect anyway because God still has me*.  Imperfections and all.  He still holds them in the palm of his hand.  This...this is the lesson that carries on from one journey to another.  To think any other way is to climb back in that same hospital window I sat in three years ago, stare again at people walking in and out, and yell at the top of my mind, "Don't come in, it's not safe!  Turn back!  Everything's going to fall apart in here!"  But it's not three years ago.  It's today.

There's another reason this chapter is hard to write.

It assumes that celebration is a universal outcome for all who experience suffering. We were fortunate enough to reach the point where we could embrace and rejoice in Luke's good health. I remember sitting in my truck in a mall parking lot, holding my face in my hands, and finally giving myself permission to cry tears of joy. They weren't the tears that had come before, when Luke was diagnosed or when I held him down to access his port. They weren't the tears of confusion when asked if I was ready for life to be normal again. They were tears of happiness and gratitude. All I could do was say, "Thank you God! Thank you so much. I was so scared. Thank you...even though it hurt!" But what about those whose loved ones didn't have the same result? What about people who had to watch their children pass away, whose tears are still ones of sorrow? How can I rejoice in the triumph and not alienate them from the celebration? I worried about this chapter. I wonder even now as I write it, where are you in your journey, and how will the ending of this story resonate with your own?

Sure, I can say some reassuring words, point out the universal nature of suffering, and talk about how the lessons God gives apply to all of us regardless of circumstance or outcome. But in the end, I didn't have to walk the whole mile in the shoes some others have had to wear. What right do I have to say anything? I've spent ten chapters talking about the experience of suffering that is common to all mankind, and the victory that is found in the redemptive hand of God. But now I am left with chapter eleven. The celebration of an outcome that has not been a universal experience for all in the journey of suffering. Not yet anyway.

And with that, I am reminded of someone who has worn those shoes. One who walked the whole mile in them, and continues to even today. I remember the words of a grieving mother who, in her efforts to find healing for herself, had the inspiration to say to me, "Luke is meant to be healed here. Eva was meant to be healed in heaven." Sadie. A parent who has not outgrown those shoes and finds them still a fit for the journey. I think about what hope means for her. I think about her and a day still to come...when she stares into the face of her daughter and her God...holds her head in her hands and cries out with tears of joy, "Thank you God! Thank you so much...even though it hurt!" There will be celebration. With hands raised, there will be rejoicing. And until that day comes, she tastes redemption every time she picks up her new baby boy, David, who taught her that she can still love the same way again. There IS redemption.

Yes, I think our stories, yours and mine, though different and unique in their own right, will find some overlap in the common struggle we call life. It's part of the human story. Somewhere in that overlap, as our hands brush by one another's, our palms will unite and rise up together. And over them all, like a parent joining the hand of one child to the other, we will see the hand of God together.

My father told me once a long time ago, "My life has had both triumphs and tragedies. And I am grateful for them both." Roughly twenty years later I came home from a grueling hospital stay, looked through a slideshow of Luke's baby pictures and cried out, "Lord, teach us how to live with this!" He taught us more. He taught us how to live.

The summer before I started high school, my father gave me a poem that is said to be written by General Douglas MacArthur, though the source is unknown. He laminated it on card stock and marked the date on the back. I wonder if he even remembers giving it to me? Either way, it had a profound effect. I saved it and have it hanging on my office wall to this day. The poem is called, "A Father's Prayer."

> Build me a son, O Lord, who will be strong enough to know when he is weak, and brave enough to face himself when he is afraid; one who will be proud and unbending in honest defeat, and humble and gentle in victory.

> Build me a son whose wishbone will not be where his backbone should be; a son who will know Thee and that to know himself is the foundation stone of knowledge. Lead him, I pray, not in the path of ease and comfort, but under the stress and spur of difficulties and challenge. Here let him learn to stand up in the storm; here let him learn compassion for those who fail.

> Build me a son whose heart will be clean, whose goal will be high; a son who will master himself before he seeks to master other men; one who will learn to laugh, yet never forget how to weep; one who will reach into the future, yet never forget the past.

> And after all these things are his, add, I pray, enough of a sense of humor, so that he may always be serious, yet never take himself too seriously. Give him humility, so that he may always remember the simplicity of greatness, the open mind of true wisdom,

the meekness of true strength.

> -General Douglas MacArthur
> (source unknown)

As a son, I strive for these virtues. I do my best to live them out. Sometimes I get it right, and other times I miss the mark entirely. But my greatest joy as I read this poem is not about me as a son anymore. I come to it now as a father, young and inexperienced, with the same prayer for my sons that my father had for me. It's a prayer for all my boys equally, but over the past few years I've been privileged to see it in light of my son Luke's fight with leukemia. I look at the way he tackled it with courage and determination, facing himself when he was afraid. How he stood up in the storm, and found compassion for those along the way. I think of this poem, then I look at Luke, and I can already dare to whisper under my breath -

...I have not lived in vain.

# Works Cited

"ἀποβάλλω." *https://accordance.bible/link/read/ BDAG#6332*

*Field of Dreams.* Directed by Phil Alden Robinson, Universal Pictures, 21 April 1989.

*The Holy Bible*, English Standard Version, Crossway, 2001.

Mad Season. *Above.* Columbia Records, 1995. CD.

"Redeem." *Merriam-Webster.com*. Merriam-Webster, 2019. Web. 3 January 2019.

# About the Author

Ryan J. Bradley was born in Bangor, Maine, in 1975, but grew up in various places throughout New England. The son of a pastor, he was raised in a Christian home, but spent years wrestling with the faith to make it his own. After being accepted into a top 25 graduate school for business administration, the growing discontent and need for discovery brought him to the sea, where he worked on various boats traveling throughout the Caribbean looking for some evidence of meaning and a relationship with God. Eventually these pursuits led him into ministry as well, where he served as a pastor and church planter for 14 years before taking leave to help his son recover and rehabilitate from a battle with meningitis and leukemia that left him disabled. Having watched this battle up close, Ryan's relationship with God became more personal than he ever imagined. A musician, author, and preacher, his work is multi-faceted in showing the need for a deeper relationship with God. Currently, he has two albums listed under the band name Wayfaring Soul and plays and preaches in New England where he still resides.

www.ingramcontent.com/pod-product-compliance
Lightning Source LLC
Chambersburg PA
CBHW030329080526
44584CB00012B/783